Genealogies of Antifascism

D.Z. Shaw

KER
SPL
EBE
DEB
2024

Genealogies of Antifascism:
Militancy, Critique, and the Three Way Fight
by D.Z. Shaw
ISBN 978-1-989701-36-2

First printing

Kersplebedeb Publishing and Distribution
CP 63560
CCCP Van Horne
Montreal, Quebec
Canada H3W 3H8

info@kersplebedeb.com
www.kersplebedeb.com
www.leftwingbooks.net

Contents

Preface

In the spring of 2003, I spoke at the Montreal Anarchist Bookfair. My talk, entitled "Strange Bedfellows?," represented an early attempt to articulate a set of new ideas that a loose circle of North American antifascists had begun to explore in the twenty short months since the 9/11 attacks. Notably, I never used the phrase "three way fight," because that terminology was still in its infancy, but one basic insight of my presentation was that "to be successful anti-fascists means being revolutionary anti-fascists, and to be revolutionary anti-fascists means being steadfast advocates and practitioners of freedom, creativity, cooperation, resistance, and diversity."[1] The intervening two decades, notwithstanding the forever wars, the rise of Obama, Trump's presidency and post-presidency, the escalating climate crisis, COVID-19, George Floyd's murder, the US Supreme Court's reversal of *Roe v. Wade*, and the currently ongoing devastation in Gaza, have done nothing to undermine the basic impulse that animated the Three Way Fight at its inception.

D.Z. Shaw, as the essays in this book make clear, shares these commitments, and he is dedicated to thinking deeply about how to justify and enact them in our present circumstances. His skills are well suited to the task, and this is an almost endlessly thought-provoking book. My limited objectives here are to highlight a couple of examples of Shaw's most powerful insights, to flag some significant potential disagreements between his perspective and my own, and to prompt readers (you!) to consider a set of guiding questions to draw on while making your way through — and beyond — this book.

POWERFUL INSIGHTS

Shaw deftly fashions a series of theoretical tools which together can (re)shape our understanding of the far right and our opposition to it. For instance, in his "Seven Theses on the Three Way Fight," he conceptualizes (especially in Theses 3 and 4) "lines of adjacency" among the three primary forces in struggle — militant antifascists, the insurgent far right, and the capitalist state. He notes that these relationships cannot be reduced to simple antagonism, that they also contain elements of ideological proximity. Thus, he points to "the line of adjacency between militant antifascism and the egalitarian aspirations of bourgeois democracy," and to "a common interest in defending settler-state hegemony against challenges from the revolutionary left and the liberation struggles of oppressed peoples [that] forms the basis of the line of adjacency" between the far right and the state. Finally, it should be clear that the line of adjacency between militant antifascists and the far right consists of the ways both "are insurgent forms of opposition against bourgeois democracy," notwithstanding the utterly incompatible visions of new societies their respective hoped-for insurrections might help produce.

Second, in a different register, Shaw has a striking ability to disentangle theoretical confusion (often caused by dependence on political jargon) that can complicate left analysis. A prime example here can be found in his essay "Revisiting *Antifascism Against Machismo*," a review of Tammy Kovich's pivotal text along with several other essays written in response. In discussing the sometimes divergent perspectives in the collection, Shaw explains that "the different participants in this intergenerational dialogue adhere to (at least) two different views of settler colonialism." He suggests that contributing author and long-time revolutionary Butch Lee sees settlerism as a particular manifestation of the complicated history of European colonialism, in which multiple and sometimes overlapping oppressed nations battle for their liberation (an approach Shaw labels "old school"), while others, including contributing author and Montreal-based revolutionary Veronica L., understand the term to describe a very specific Indigenous/settler binary; Shaw calls this a "new school" approach, and he seems to situate himself in its orbit, while carefully assessing the problems he finds in it.

As I read, I discerned that my own analysis — shaped largely through links of solidarity with revolutionary elements of the Puerto Rican diaspora in the United States — is closer to the "old school." I find Shaw's distinction helpful in articulating my own concerns about some of the ways in which much current left discourse on settler colonialism seems to elide or flatten many complexities of race and nation in colonial contexts. I've long been supremely grateful for the relative handful of encounters I had with Lee before she passed away in 2021, and now I'm thankful for Shaw's helpful disambiguation, which extends her powerful legacy. Butch Lee, ¡presente!

POTENTIAL DISAGREEMENTS

Lee and her life-long comrade J. Sakai are part of a set of common intellectual influences Shaw and I share, as are other revolutionary writers from W.E.B. DuBois to Don Hamerquist. That he and I draw sometimes different conclusions from the same sources speaks nicely to the open-ended and evolving character of the Three Way Fight as a framework for understanding revolutionary social change in the twenty-first century.

That said, there are places in this book where I find Shaw's arguments less than compelling. This is particularly the case in the book's previously unpublished essay, "Why Judith Butler is Wrong about Militant Antifascism," which strikes me as often too abstract, sometimes muddled, and occasionally tendentious.

Shaw criticizes Butler's advocacy for nonviolent models of social change and their attempt to caution against antifascist violence, as when they argue that "the actualization of violence as a means can inadvertently become its own end, producing new violence, producing violence anew, reiterating the license, and licensing further violence."[2] Without defending Butler's work in this area, with which I'm not especially familiar, I want to note that their concerns about the dangerous if unintended consequences of violent actions by antifascists are entirely well founded in light of the recent history of militant antifascist efforts, particularly in the context of Anti-Racist Action (ARA) during the period between the mid-1980s and the early twenty-first century.

I'll offer just one example among many contained in *We Go Where They Go: The Story of Anti-Racist Action.* In reflecting on one of the most violent periods described in the book, long-time Skinheads Against Racial Prejudice (SHARP) and ARA organizer Eric from Cincinnati explains in detail how, in a local struggle between anti-racist and neo-nazi skinheads during the late 1980s, "the violence increased … escalating over time [as] both sides collected trophies, carrying razors to cut the laces of beaten rivals and take their boots."[3] Certainly no pacifist, Eric nonetheless soberly analyzes his own post-ARA struggles resulting from "the violence I did to others. That's what keeps me up at night. The thing is these are fellow human beings that are an existential threat to you, but they are human beings, right?"[4] Other veterans of ARA have shared comparable experiences including PTSD, suicide, substance dependency, and intergenerational trauma, all of which would seem to provide evidence for the validity of Butler's stated concern. The lesson here is not that antifascists should abandon violence entirely — Eric argues compellingly that this would have been suicidal in the context he describes — but that they must be attentive to the unintended yet predictable consequences of their actions, and that it is imperative to develop strategies to address these.

One such strategy, as described repeatedly in *We Go Where They Go*, is to use the threat of violence to prevent actual violence. Here again, Butler appears to be on more solid ground than Shaw is willing to acknowledge. He attributes to them the claim that "superior numbers" have allowed antifascists to successfully challenge public-facing far-right activity, highlighting the specific example of Milo Yiannopoulos's contentious appearance at the University of California in early 2017, where more than a thousand protesters helped shut down the event. *Contra* Butler, Shaw maintains that "a superior number of counterprotesters is neither necessary nor sufficient for undermining far-right organizing." On its face, this statement is undeniably true, and yet another core lesson to be drawn from the experience of ARA is that it "was prepared for militant confrontation, but most importantly, directly mobilized and worked alongside great numbers of people, especially locals, standing up against racism."[5] In this sense, strategic considerations for ARA strongly suggested that violence should be avoided when it *could* be avoided, and that one key way to avoid it was to outnumber the fascists in the streets.

This may in fact be another "old-school/new-school" sort of disagreement, as Shaw's argument likely resonates with a generation of militant antifascists that has, in the years since 9/11, prioritized smaller, sometimes semi-clandestine, cell-like organizing structures. The massive expansion of the surveillance state in the early twenty-first century undeniably justified this shift, but the explosion in far-right organizing over the past decade just as certainly highlights its fundamental limitations. Butler may overstate the case, but superior numbers can and do contribute to antifascist victories.

GUIDING QUESTIONS

This book is being published in confusing, difficult, and, indeed, scary times. It will undoubtedly be generative reading for a cross-section of antifascists and revolutionaries. To make the most of it, I suggest that those who engage with these writings keep the following questions in mind:

▶ What role do long-standing left categories of analysis like race, gender, and class play in developing sophisticated theories of militant antifascism, particularly when each of them necessarily complicates the apparent simplicity of the Three Way Fight framework?

▶ How should radicals understand and act upon the co-constitutive relationship between revolutionary theory and antifascist strategy in a world undergoing profound transformations at incredible speed?

▶ Since, following Shaw, it is crucial to "recognize and uphold the 'revolutionary horizon' of antifascist struggle [such that] fascism cannot be permanently defeated until the conditions that give rise to fascism are overthrown," how can militant antifascists help encourage a mass popular embrace of this horizon among a broad cross-section of people?

If these questions don't speak to you, come up with your own. As I regularly tell students, questions can be more valuable than answers; they remind us that the world is not unalterably stuck in its current (horrifically damaged) state, that the way forward is not fixed. Read this book, and work collectively with comrades to envision a revolutionary horizon, and to chart a militant antifascist path toward it.

Michael Staudenmaier
Chicago, April 2024

NOTES

1. As of April, 2024, the text of this talk, initially published in *The Fifth Estate* in 2003, is still available online at: https://www.fifthestate.org/archive/361-summer-2003-2/strange-bedfellows/. Note also that weeks before, I had co-authored the BRICK Anarchist Collective's discussion document, "Above and Below: Them, Them and Us," which includes the earliest usage of the phrase "three way fight" in an antifascist context; that document is available in Xtn Alexander and Matthew N. Lyons, eds., *Three Way Fight: Revolutionary Politics and Antifascism* (PM Press/Kersplebedeb, 2024), 37–43.

2. Judith Butler, *The Force of Nonviolence: An Ethico-Political Bind* (London: Verso, 2020), 20.

3. Shannon Clay et al., *We Go Where They Go: The Story of Anti-Racist Action* (Oakland: PM Press, 2023), 24–25.

4. Clay, et al., *We Go Where They Go*, 265.

5. Clay, et al., *We Go Where They Go*, 263.

Introduction

This book collects a selection of essays I've written on fascism and antifascism, all but one published between January 2020 and fall of 2023. Many are occasional pieces responding to contemporary events or reviewing books. Even the few that I would categorize as deliberate interventions on theoretical or practical issues were motivated by a growing literature on militant antifascism. All were written as the socio-political terrain of North America shifted in several unprecedented directions.

When I first engaged with *Antifascism Against Machismo*, by Tammy Kovich (then writing as Petronella Lee), or Jason Stanley's *How Fascism Works* during the fall of 2019 and winter of 2020, the battle lines between antifascists and far-right movements were clearly drawn, such that street battles between them in places like Portland, Oregon, risked being ritualized and/or managed by the police. I taught those works, among others, to a third-year seminar within a social context that had developed and solidified between 2016 and 2020, which was quickly upended by the COVID-19 pandemic, the anti-police (or "George Floyd") uprising in summer 2020, the electoral defeat of Donald Trump and the far-right putsch of January 6, 2021, the so-called Freedom Convoy protests in Canada in 2022, and finally, in 2023, a shift and retrenchment of far-right organizing that aimed at deepening a moral panic about the existence of transgender and queer folks.

These writings are intended for a politically committed, theoretically inclined activist audience. In general, the essays collected herein are reproduced very close to their original form. Some changes address instances where there was lack of clarity that the publisher and I felt could be corrected. Others are stylistic, which I consider instances where some clumsy academic circumlocutions have been unravelled. I have minimized the scope of revisions, however, so that these chapters can better reflect snapshots of a philosophy of antifascism in motion, one that attempts to think through the theoretical and practical ramifications of the treacherous political terrain of the last few years.

In Part I, I have included three essays that introduce and address theoretical topics in militant antifascism. In Chapter 1, I outline and defend seven theses on the three way fight. In Chapter 2, I apply this theoretical framework to interpret the phenomenon of vigilantism during the anti-police uprising of 2020. In Chapter 3, I use the theses on the three way fight to critique the orthodox line upheld by Dimitrov in *The Fascist Offensive*, which remains at the basis of many Marxist conceptions of fascism. In the epilogue to Chapter 3, I pick up the red thread of an alternative genealogy of revolutionary antifascism, one which shows how Lenin's analyses of the formation of a European labor aristocracy within the imperialist system and W.E.B. Du Bois's discussion of "the wages of whiteness" suggest themes that were later taken up by theorists of the three way fight.

Part II collects occasional pieces that cover—as the chapter titles tend to indicate—militant feminist antifascism, the critique of liberal antifascism, the use of the Black Radical Tradition in antifascist theory, a critique of Brahmanism, and the history of German communist antifascist resistance. In the review of Shane Burley's *Why We Fight*, which also covers some of these themes, there is an extended examination of the class character of far-right movements.

Part III consists of one essay, "Why Judith Butler is Wrong about Militant Antifascism," which is being published here for the first time. Butler is an important public philosopher whose work warrants an in-depth critical analysis, for it expresses the contradictions and anxieties of liberal antifascism and nonviolent resistance. In *The Force of Nonviolence*, they argue that a concern for care, grievability, and vulnerability necessitates the use of nonviolent forms of resistance and world-building. I argue, drawing on the work of Simone de Beauvoir, that such concerns could also justify the use of what I call emancipatory community self-defense. Butler refuses to recognize emancipatory community self-defense as a legitimate form of militant organizing that is, both philosophically and practically, fundamentally different from common-sense notions of self-defense. I show that Butler's critique of militant antifascism ultimately rests on the mistaken assertion that the use of emancipatory violence by the left licenses the far right to escalate with further violence.

While these essays range over a number of topics, they share some important themes in common. First and foremost, I outline and defend a three way fight approach to militant antifascism. I have summarized the development of this approach in the introduction to Chapter 3, "Notes for a Critique of Dimitrov." For the moment, it will suffice to say that the three way fight rejects the orthodox Marxist (and sometimes anarchist) definition of fascism as a politics or policy of the most reactionary elements of the bourgeoisie. Instead, advocates of the three way fight hold that revolutionary antifascist movements must struggle on two fronts: against capitalism and its attendant forms of liberalism and social-democratic reformism *and* against far-right movements that are system-oppositional at the same time as they seek to re-entrench certain forms systemic oppression. Given that I write in a North American context, these include capitalism, white supremacy, heteropatriarchy, ableism, and settler colonialism.

Second, I defend militant antifascism against liberal antifascism. *Militant antifascism*, in my view, entails at least two commitments: first, it is a form of community self-defense that embraces a diversity of tactics in order to combat far-right and fascist organizing within our communities; second, it holds that antifascist organizing must be responsive to a "revolutionary horizon" of struggle that acknowledges that fascism cannot be permanently defeated until the conditions which give rise to it are overthrown. *Liberal antifascism*, by contrast, aims to fight fascism through the inculcation of stronger democratic norms, the free exchange of ideas in the public sphere, and the reinforcement of liberal institutions of government. Mark Bray describes these beliefs as a kind of "faith," and if the years from 2016 to 2020 tested liberal antifascists' faith in public institutions and democratic norms, the events of the last few years have also tested their faith that law enforcement and the whole repressive state apparatus will throw their weight behind the liberal institutions of government. Nonetheless, I return time and again, from the first chapter to the last, to a critique of liberal antifascism. Liberal antifascism remains resilient, and it has proven its resilience, not through faith, but through pragmatism, shoring itself up by vacillating between socio-political doubt—which temporarily widens the space for militant organizing to maneuver—and support for liberal hegemonic blocs.

A commitment to the three way fight and militant antifascism guides my approach. Many of these writings are motivated by the concern that as militant antifascist work ebbs—and it seems to be at a low ebb, at least momentarily—that it cedes organizational and discursive ground to liberal antifascism. Which means that antifascism in theory and practice will encounter several problems that will hinder organizing work, i.e., hinder antifascist organizing to undermine far-right movements. Therefore, part of the defense of militant antifascism involves identifying the weaknesses of liberal antifascism. Throughout this book, I explore two of these weaknesses. First, liberal antifascism tends to treat fascism as a rhetorical or political strategy to gain institutional power; hence, it upholds the mistaken belief that fascism can be defeated by electoral or parliamentarian mechanisms. Second, as with many tendencies within liberalism (such as social democracy), it operates within a reformist political paradigm that precludes exploring how to extirpate the conditions that give rise to fascism, such as the capitalist mode of production or settler colonialism.

In the final chapter, I explore the inability of liberal antifascism to resolve its ambivalence toward violence, law enforcement, and self-defense. This is most evident in the fact that many discussions about self-defense rely on a "common-sense notion" that conceives of self-defense as an exceptional moment within a political continuum that runs from individual right to state violence. According to this notion, the individual assumes that they are protected by law enforcement; but, when there is an "imminent threat" and law enforcement is not present, an individual has the natural or self-evident right to protect their person, property, and family. In the final chapter of this book, I propose and defend a concept of "emancipatory community self-defense," a practice that fosters autonomy and solidarity for socially vulnerable groups. Emancipatory community self-defense is organized against the antagonism of police oppression, so there is no presumed continuum between community action and police power. Significantly, this communal form of self-defense is often not protected by the "right" to self-defense extended by the state. The liberal approach denies the legitimacy of emancipatory community self-defense, and in so doing it undermines one of the most important aspects of antifascist organizing: building and maintaining solidarity with embattled communities that face violence and antagonism from both the repressive apparatus of the state and the far right. For without autonomous community self-defense organizing, where would these communities turn when threatened by the far right, other than to an already antagonistic state power? In my view, liberal antifascism is only able to direct embattled communities back to an already antagonistic law enforcement that subjects them to increased social vulnerability. While, admittedly, militant antifascist groups have been criticized for their failures in organizing with embattled communities, a revolutionary theory of antifascism should clearly defend the use of emancipatory community self-defense.

Aside from these themes, the essays collected in this book also share a common theoretical horizon. They were all written after the manuscript for *Philosophy of Antifascism: Punching Nazis and Fighting White Supremacy* was finalized for publication.[1] As I reread them today, I notice that they all point toward a theoretical horizon beyond that book, and even beyond a necessarily linear history of the theory and practice of militant antifascism.

Most of my work has aimed to shift the geography of the genealogy of militant antifascism from the history of fascism in Europe to one informed by the North American context. While I think it is necessary to be fluent in the histories of European fascist movements and their international influence, and while I appreciate the authors who have worked to reconstruct the often obscure but important histories of antifascist organizing, I think that we need to dispense with the idea that there is a continuous, linear history of revolutionary antifascism. I think this point is especially evident when it comes to antifascist theory. The clearest case—which I outline in Chapter 3—involves what I would call the split between Dimitrov and Du Bois, between the orthodox communist theory that maintains that fascism is a top-down strategy led by a small, reactionary faction of the bourgeoisie, and a heterodox theory that seeks to diagnose how the far right emerges as an autonomous, potentially mass-base, system-oppositional social movement. Historically speaking, it appears that often advocates of either position did not see themselves as articulating two radically different approaches. James Boggs, for example, tried to split the difference:

> Fascism in the United States is therefore unique in that it is grass roots rather than from the top down. Today the Minute Men, America Firsters, White Citizens' Councils, and the scores of other white organizations organized to defend the United States from the demands of blacks for justice are made up of workers, skilled and unskilled, who work every day alongside

blacks in the shop and then night after night organize
in the suburbs against these same blacks.[2]

From the perspective of the development of the three way fight,
works such as Don Hamerquist and J. Sakai's contributions to
Confronting Fascism consolidated the criticisms of the orthodox
line and demonstrated the theoretical and practical importance
of reconceptualizing fascism as a system-oppositional movement—to the then contemporary American context *and* to the
history of fascism. A paradoxical system-oppositional social
movement that seeks to re-entrench the inequalities present in
that system on terms advantageous to its base. An oppressor
culture, as Sakai would say, and a particularly dangerous one
at that.

I will conclude this reflection by noting a few vantage points
that I think have yet to be fully developed.

First, when I talk about class, or when some other advocates
of the three way fight talk about it, these discussions are heavily
indebted to theorists who challenge orthodox Marxist accounts
of class, such as Sakai, Butch Lee, and Bromma, for whom
class is inextricable from race and gender. In both Chapter 3
and Chapter 9, I have outlined some preliminary remarks on the
class composition of the (potential) mass base for fascism. More
work is necessary here. Already in *Confronting Fascism*, part of
Sakai's essay questions whether or not he and Hamerquist are
using similar class categories. It would be interesting to summarize the trajectory of Sakai's, Lee's, and Bromma's analyses
of class over time, in order to bridge discussions of antifascism
with their non-conventional Marxist theories of class (to which
I adhere far more closely than orthodox class categories), race,
gender, and settler colonialism.

Second, as a consequence, we will need to revisit the differences between the theories of oppressed nations and internal colonialism—discussions which were framed and
grounded in Black liberation movement readings of Marxism-
Leninism from the 1960s—and contemporary concepts of

settler colonialism, which I only began to broach in Chapter 10, "Revisiting *Antifascism against Machismo.*"

Finally, it seems more and more evident—as Tammy Kovich and Butch Lee emphasize—that contemporary far-right movements are built heavily around varying degrees of misogyny and transphobia and not merely racism. Although the far right in 2024 does not seem to be organizing for direct confrontation with antifascists along the lines of 2016–2020, certain elements do seem to be attempting to mainstream far-right views through transphobic organizing. This is a worrying development, given the prevalence of transphobia in mainstream culture. Here, in a sense, is an example of the far right seeking to re-entrench gender hierarchies on terms conducive to its male supremacist outlook. But due to the considerable mainstream acceptance of heteropatriarchy, far-right participation in sowing moral panics or protesting "gender ideology" looks less like system-oppositional *far-right* organizing than it does merely system-loyal right-wing organizing. In my view, the stakes are high, for I would argue that this moral panic is only one part of a broader strategy for attacking the bodily autonomy of anybody who isn't a cisgendered, white man. We need a contemporary line of sight into the relationship between mainstream and far-right heteropatriarchy, but we should also use this perspective to look back at the history of far-right attitudes toward women, gender, and sexuality. It's not by accident that the last chapter in Part II revisits the themes I covered in the first: fascism, antifascism, feminism, and heteropatriarchy.

The questions that arise when we consider fascism and antifascism in relation to class, settler colonialism, and heteropatriarchy warrant further exploration. I hope that the writing I've done over the last few years—in tandem with the anthology edited by Xtn Alexander and Matthew N. Lyons, *Three Way Fight: Revolutionary Politics and Antifascism* (published by PM Press and Kersplebedeb)—helps move those discussions forward.

NOTES

1. D.Z. Shaw, *Philosophy of Antifascism: Punching Nazis and Fighting White Supremacy* (London: Rowman and Littlefield International, 2020).

2. James Boggs, *Racism and the Class Struggle: Further Pages from a Black Worker's Notebook* (New York: Monthly Review Press, 1970), 96.

I. The Three Way Fight

1. Seven Theses on the Three Way Fight

In leftist—that is, socialist, anarchist, and communist—circles, it is still common to hear discussions of fascism couched in terms similar to Dimitrov's formulation of the Comintern's Popular Front line as established in 1935. He asserts that "fascism in power is the open terrorist dictatorship of the most reactionary, most chauvinistic and most imperialist elements of finance capital."[1] The prolonged afterlife of this definition is likely due in part to the fact that it was later adopted, with slight modification, by the Black Panther Party in its call for a United Front against Fascism in 1969: "Fascism is the open terroristic dictatorship of the most reactionary, most chauvinistic (racist) and the most imperialist elements of finance capital."[2] Though I readily accept that fascism must be understood as a movement that is enabled by and is a reaction to capitalist crises, and I maintain that fascism cannot take power without some factions of capital collaborating with far-right movements, there are numerous problems with identifying its overriding class character with the most extreme factions of capital. If we re-examine Dimitrov's two major essays from 1935—"The Fascist Offensive and the Tasks of the Communist International in the Struggle of the Working

---

The seven theses I propose here were first published as part of the preface to T. Derbent's *German Communist Resistance 1933–1945*, published by Foreign Languages Press (2021). I was then invited to rework parts of that preface as a standalone essay that was first published on the *Three Way Fight* website, August 1, 2021.

Class against Fascism" and "Unity of the Working Class against Fascism"—we find that his analysis hints at a more complicated picture of the class character of fascism, even while it is largely explained away as a product of demagoguery.[3] In any case, from this overarching perspective, the non-bourgeois elements of fascist movements are treated as mere instruments or lackeys of the fascist bourgeoisie.

Some critics reject the orthodox Marxist line represented by Dimitrov but nonetheless preserve part of its form: where Dimitrov focuses on the specific *class character* of fascism—that is, locating its leadership within the most reactionary and extreme factions of the bourgeoisie—this non-orthodox interpretation treats fascism as an extreme version of some aspects of capitalist *social relations*. In other words, while Dimitrov focuses on fascism as a particularly extreme and terroristic form of one particular faction of bourgeois class rule, these critics treat fascism as a new particular application of the state's repressive apparatuses. These critics also overstate how contemporary fascism breaks from patterns of classical fascism: Enzo Traverso's "postfascism," Samir Gandesha's "posthuman fascism," or Alberto Toscano's "racial fascism" (which evokes a parallel to the concept of racial capitalism, but adding "racial" to fascism is redundant) or "late fascism."[4] Fascism, though, is not merely a new phase of capitalism or state repression.

These variations on the thesis that fascism represents an extreme faction or policy of capitalism all fall short for the same reason: they do not reflect the reality on the ground, in the concrete struggle between militant antifascism and far-right and fascist movements. It's clearly not the bourgeoisie who were holding the tiki torches in Charlottesville. And while there are connections and ideological similarities between the far right and certain apparatuses of state power (such as the police), their organizational interests do not necessarily align. In sum, the received concept of fascism as an extreme faction or policy of capitalism does not explain the presence of system-oppositional currents within the far right that fight against bourgeois political and cultural power. (Which is different than saying bourgeois class rule; as I argue in Theses 2 and 5, far-right movements seek to reorganize capital accumulation on terms advantageous to their base, not to overthrow capitalism.) Indeed, these Dimitrov variations, as it were, could each lend themselves to a supposed leftist argument against using direct action: if fascism is the product of the most reactionary elements of the class rule of capital or an extreme implementation of repressive state power, the argument would go, then using direct action against the far-right malcontents in the streets siphons resources from broader anticapitalist organizing. In other words, from this perspective, militant antifascism would combat symptoms rather than causes.

Hence, from a militant perspective, there is a need for a different approach. Unsurprisingly, there has been a growing interest in the history and practice of nonorthodox approaches to antifascist organizing; for example, the 43 Group, the John Brown Anti-Klan Committee (JBAKC), Anti-Racist Action (ARA), and, as evidenced by the re-edition of the anthology *Confronting Fascism* in 2017, the three way fight (although unlike the aforementioned groups, the three way fight is not an organization as such).[5] These sometimes had similar approaches, but we must also highlight their differences. The three way fight differs from the others because, despite the organizational, extra-legal, and militant aspects of these groupings and movements, they did not develop the necessary revolutionary outlook to orient their activity.[6] Even within ARA, the revolutionary concepts which formed the basis for the three way fight position were a minority tendency. What is needed now are the revolutionary, liberatory visions and living forms of praxis of the three way fight. I will tentatively define the three way fight, which I will outline in more detail below, as an approach to antifascist struggle that situates militant action against both system-oppositional far-right groups and bourgeois democracy (as it is embodied, in North America, in both bourgeois democratic institutions and in what I call settler-state hegemony, liberalism as ideology, and the repressive state apparatus). Reality on the ground is more complicated and rife with contradictions than a one-sentence definition can encapsulate, so while this tentative definition cannot replace the seven theses I propose below, it does serve as a starting point for the discussion.

THE PRESENT CONJUNCTURE

Before presenting the seven theses on the three way fight, I want to underline that, compared to the last five years, the co-ordinates of antifascist struggle have changed. While militant antifascism is best known for its embrace of a diversity of tactics, over the past several years many militants have worked to create a broader social atmosphere of "everyday antifascism," which brought those whom I would call "liberal antifascists" into the broader struggle against far-right groups. Fostering everyday antifascism makes it possible to organize a broader movement in opposition to far-right groups when they mobilize in our communities. Everyday antifascism could, under the right conditions, bring larger crowds to counter-protests; it also provides political education on how the seemingly small things, like seating far-right groups at restaurants or providing lodging, enable the far-right threat. Although Trump would never promote antifascism as a form of system-loyal American civic participation, it was promoted by some who opposed to him, e.g., as election day approached, intellectuals such as Cornel West described their support for Biden as an "antifascist vote." A united front of militant antifascists—largely drawn from socialist, communist, and anarchist backgrounds—was formed within a broader milieu that included sympathetic liberal antifascists who, if they were not themselves drawn toward militant action, at least provided room to maneuver.

With Trump deposed from power, the situation has changed. The differences between liberal antifascists and militants are more starkly illuminated as the immediate threat—cr what was perceived by some as the immediate threat—of fascism has abated. Thus, we should reiterate the differences between these two currents of antifascism:

▶ *Militant antifascism* upholds a diversity of tactics to combat far-right and fascist organizing; it organizes as a form of community self-defense which (at least ideally) builds reciprocal relationships with marginalized and oppressed communities. In addition, it ought to recognize and uphold the "revolutionary horizon" of antifascist struggle: fascism cannot be permanently defeated until the conditions that give rise to fascism are overthrown.

▶ *Liberal antifascism*, in Mark Bray's concise definition, entails "a faith in the inherent power of the public sphere to filter out fascist ideas, and in the institutions of government to forestall the advancement of fascist politics."[7] Liberal antifascists appeal to the democratic norms of these institutions, but they also assume that law enforcement will apply force to repress fascism when it constitutes a legitimate threat; furthermore, they also tend to accept the converse of the foregoing proposition: if law enforcement doesn't intervene, then no legitimate threat is present.

In the wake of the attempted far-right putsch on Capitol Hill on January 6, 2021, when I was working on the first version of this essay, I suggested that the Biden administration was poised to marshal the popular outrage toward that event to siphon parts of the broader atmosphere of everyday antifascism—which previously made it possible to organize militant antifascist actions relatively openly—to fortify Democratic blocs.[8] Biden had, for example, in August 2017, only a few weeks after the Unite the Right rally in Charlottesville, published an editorial in *The Atlantic* denouncing Trump's equivocations about the far right; he had also referenced Charlottesville several times during his campaign. However, as it turns out, mainstream liberal antifascists were content to encapsulate and isolate fascism around so-called "Trumpism," which was allegedly defeated with the victory and inauguration of the Biden administration—though, they sternly warned, a more effective demagogue could wreak more havoc than Trump in the future.

We must, by contrast, disentangle an array of far-right phenomena: Trump's particular propaganda campaign against the legitimacy of his electoral defeat; the drift, or push, of the Republican Party toward far-right ideology; Trump's attempt to suppress the 2020 anti-police uprising; and the temporary realignment of ideologically system-oppositional groups as system-loyal vigilantism against antifascist and anti-racist organizing. What differentiates our perspective from the critique of "Trumpism," and what we must emphasize, is that we cannot lose sight of the fact that the far right is a relatively autonomous social movement. Trump's ascendency was based in part on the emergence and growth of far-right organizing, but he certainly didn't conjure these forces out of the blue. Likewise, his 2020 electoral defeat does not signal their defeat and dissolution.

In order to examine the present conjuncture, we must admit that the coalitions between militant and liberal antifascists that have formed over the last five years (2016–21) were fraught from the beginning. The two tendencies adhere to incompatible ideological commitments and organizational strategies. As previously noted, militant antifascists struggle against both the far right *and* bourgeois democracy. This dual struggle necessitates criticism of liberal antifascism as well. First, militant antifascists, as I argue in Thesis 6, must maintain a revolutionary horizon, in which their practices are directed toward not only fighting the far right, but forging the organizational capacity and skills for a broader social—and in its various manifestations, also class—struggle against capitalist rule. This struggle brings antifascist action into direct conflict with both the far right and the state's repressive apparatus, and hence militants must carry out investigations into the relationship between law enforcement and far-right organizing. Liberal perspectives and militant perspectives will never align on law enforcement.

But as militant and liberal antifascist coalitions fragment, we must also pay close attention to the vicissitudes of liberal antifascism. In the interregnum between January 6, 2021, and the Inauguration, some liberal antifascists framed American civic participation and protection of democratic institutions as antifascist; this is the basis on which I had previously examined the potential for Biden to appropriate similar discourse. As it turns out, Biden's administration pivoted—not unlike numerous liberal antifascist intellectuals—from formulating an opposition of antifascism and fascism to an opposition between liberal norms and extremism. We must interpret this pivot.

Given that liberal antifascists rely on democratic norms and rational persuasion to criticize fascist positions, under normal circumstances they carry out criticism within the parameters of liberal institutions, especially through the medium of intellectual exchange and debate. And under normal conditions, liberal ideology writ large—and liberal antifascists as a whole are typically no exception—condemns insurgent organizing, whether it is of the militant left or the far right, as political "extremism" (patterned on the discourse of so-called totalitarianism, which equivocates between communism and fascism). Hence liberal horseshoe theory, which empties fascism and militant antifascism of their explicit (and incompatible) political content in order to present them as two iterations of purportedly irrational violence, even though, of course, the only thing the two share is the rejection of the state's asserted monopoly on violence.

But when the far right mounts a significant challenge to bourgeois political and cultural power, threatening liberal institutions, and (unsurprisingly) intellectual exchange and debate prove ineffective, some liberal antifascists enter into coalitions with or within militant groups. We saw numerous instances of this over the last few years. Though there are pronounced theoretical and practical differences between them, these two currents of antifascism converge around a shared sense of egalitarianism, which opens for militants a broader horizon for organizing around the practices of everyday antifascism. As a consequence of this practical readjustment, we have seen liberal antifascists set aside the framework of "extremism" in order to enter the struggle between militant antifascism and the far right.

However, when the threat of fascism seems to have passed—that is, at least from the liberal perspective, when it appears that the far right has failed to seize political, cultural, or institutional control—we should expect, and must prepare for, liberal antifascism to revert to its normal institutional habits. Thus, just as liberalism shores up political hegemony, liberal antifascism returns to the paradigm of "extremism" in order to categorize militant and revolutionary leftist movements and the far right as two sides of the same extremist coin. I believe we are witnessing these shifts at the present moment, and hence it is all the more important that antifascist intellectuals both critique and refuse to collaborate with those think tanks and university institutions that push the "extremism studies" approach to fascism and antifascism. An academic pedigree for parts of the state security apparatus does not remove their ultimately repressive function.

When liberal antifascists categorize militant antifascism as extremist, they not only work to delegitimize militant currents, they also provide repressive state apparatuses with an ideological justification for the political use of force. If liberal antifascism succeeds in pulling everyday antifascism back toward bourgeois forms of institutional and cultural power, it will effectively empty everyday antifascism of any concrete political and organizational content while setting the stage for state repression of militant antifascists.[9] The extension of law enforcement powers that follows in the wake of far-right actions related to the Capitol riot will rebound against left-wing militants, given that the repressive state apparatus specifically frames its work in this domain as a fight against extremism.

In my view, the political success of liberal antifascism will always be a pyrrhic victory. Militant antifascism draws its strength from its organizational capacity—that is, from its ability to undermine far-right organizing. When words no longer match deeds, when theory no longer matches practical results, then militant antifascism enters into crisis. The principal contradiction of militant antifascism is that these forms of organizing often only last as long as the threat of specific far-right groups persists.

But repressive state violence, under the auspices of fighting political extremism, can apply force to accelerate the decomposition of militant organizing capacity. Liberal antifascists do not recognize, or do not adequately challenge, how their typical political framework legitimizes state power. They do not recognize how dismantling militant antifascist organizing capacity undermines community self-defense, and hence how it enables conditions for far-right forces to regroup. The danger remains that conditions arise in the future that are even more conducive to far-right movements than they have been over the last five years.

SEVEN THESES ON MILITANT ANTIFASCISM

The foregoing scenario is far from a *fait accompli*. It can be forestalled by renewed efforts at militant political education and organizing around a united front policy. The electoral defeat of the Trump administration has untethered far-right organizing from its momentary system-loyal pretensions, though without necessarily undermining alliances that were forged by the mutual opposition of some far-right groups and police departments to the anti-police uprising of 2020. I will conclude by proposing a series of theses concerning a united front policy for militant antifascists in North America, though I believe some points also hold in other situations. We will begin with defining two terms: fascism and the far right.

1. Fascism is a social movement involving a relatively autonomous and insurgent (potentially) mass base, driven by an authoritarian vision of collective rebirth, that challenges bourgeois institutional and cultural power while re-entrenching economic and social hierarchies. This definition of fascism—adapted from the work of Matthew N. Lyons and drawing from the discussion between Don Hamerquist and J. Sakai in *Confronting Fascism* (2002)—is a marked departure from the most common Marxist definition, which holds that fascism is "the open terrorist dictatorship of the most reactionary, most chauvinistic and most imperialist elements of finance capital."[10] Whereas Dimitrov's formulation, as it is typically applied, treats fascists in the streets as instruments of the most reactionary faction of capital, the definition I offer asserts that fascist social movements are relatively autonomous formations that challenge bourgeois institutional and cultural power. This autonomy does not preclude alliances between fascists and the bourgeoisie. As Hamerquist argues, the Nazis' seizure of power united factions of the ruling class interested in imposing fascism "from above" with non-socialist factions (and I'm using the term "socialist" as loosely as possible here) of the fascist movement, and "nazi political structure had a clear and substantial autonomy from the capitalist class and the strength to impose certain positions on that class."[11]

As to the class composition of fascism, T. Derbent comments that "workers were the only social group whose percentage of Nazi party members was lower than its percentage in the total population."[12] Closer to the present, an examination of 49 of 107 persons arrested for participation in the Capitol riot indicates the generally petty bourgeois character of participants.[13] Both observations affirm that the class composition of the far right and fascism is more complex than just "the most reactionary faction(s) of the bourgeoisie." In North America, the far right draws from elements of the white petty bourgeoisie who are seeking to protect their social status—purchased, as W.E.B. Du Bois argues, through the wages of whiteness—and/or their class position. Fascism is, in my view, relatively autonomous because it is anti-bourgeois, but it is anti-capitalist only to the degree that it seeks to reorganize capital accumulation on terms more favorable to its base. To illustrate: Hamerquist has adduced examples where fascist policies have interrupted the normal functioning of capitalism, but as Lyons notes, "no fascist movement has substantively attacked core capitalist structures such as private property and the market economy."[14]

2. Fascist ideology and organizing develop within a broader far-right ecological niche.
Lyons defines the far right as inclusive of "political forces that (a) regard human inequality as natural, inevitable, or desirable and (b) reject the legitimacy of the established political system."[15] Lyons's definition focuses our attention on two key features of the far-right milieu within which fascists organize. First, far-right groups seek to re-entrench social and economic inequalities, but the social hierarchies they advocate aren't necessarily drawn along racial lines. Lyons gives the example of the Christian far right, which advocates for a theocratic state that centers heterosexual male dominance. In general, this movement has embraced Islamophobia and "promotes policies that implicitly bolster racial oppression," but some groups have conducted outreach to conservative Christians of color while others have formed alliances with white supremacist groups.[16] Fascist movements emerge within a broader milieu of right-wing social movements, and these various groups sometimes establish alliances and sometimes conflict. In fact, one purpose of antifascist counter-protesting when these groups rally is to put pressure on their organizing; when these rallies are disrupted or dispersed through antifascist action, far-right alliances often splinter as prominent figures and groups trade accusations and recriminations.

Second, far-right groups reject the legitimacy of, as I would phrase it, bourgeois-democratic institutions of political and cultural power. Though mainstream conservatism has been pulled toward the far right in ideological terms, the organizational difference between "oppositional and system-loyal rightists is more significant than ideological differences about race, religion, economics, or other factors."[17]

3. Militant antifascism is involved in a three way fight against insurgent far-right movements and bourgeois democracy (or, in ideological terms, liberalism).

More precisely, each "corner" of the three way fight struggles against the other two at the same time as this struggle offers lines of adjacency against a common enemy. The first and most fundamental lesson of the three way fight is that while both revolutionary movements and far-right movements are insurgent forms of opposition against bourgeois democracy, "my enemy's enemy is not my friend." Given that far-right groups also aim to recruit or ally with some leftist groups, it is all the more important to root out all forms of chauvinism within our practices and organizations. Second, we must recognize the line of adjacency between militant antifascism and the egalitarian aspirations of bourgeois democracy. It is the shared appeal to egalitarianism that makes fostering a broader sense of everyday antifascism possible. But this also means, as I will argue in Thesis 6, that militants must uphold a revolutionary horizon to keep the limitations of liberal antifascism in focus.

We will deal with the line of adjacency between the far right and bourgeois democracy (or liberalism) in the next two theses. But before moving on, we must examine the relationship between far-right groups and law enforcement. The slogan that "cops and klan go hand-in-hand" expresses two fundamental aspects of this relationship. First, it acknowledges the systemic role of law enforcement; that is, law enforcement protects the systemic white supremacy of North American settler-colonial states. Second, it also calls attention to not only shared membership between the two groups (when police, for example, are also members of the KKK), but also the ideological bases through which police and system-loyal vigilante groups find common cause in opposition to leftist movements and (potentially) insurgent oppressed classes and nations.

However, it would be incorrect to assume that there are no antagonisms between law enforcement and far-right groups. In my view, it is more accurate to differentiate between what I would call system-loyal vigilantism and system-oppositional armed organization. On the terms established by Lyons, all far-right groups are ideologically system-oppositional, *but not all of them are organized in system-oppositional forms*. Over the last few years, many framed their actions as system-loyal vigilantism, which I would define as the use of violent tactics to harass, intimidate, or physically harm individuals or groups participating in transformative egalitarian movements. While some levels of law enforcement tend to be permissive or deferential toward system-loyal right-wing vigilantism, there are recent examples of law enforcement at the federal level moving to repress system-oppositional groups organized around armed insurgency. In 2020, law enforcement moved to incapacitate numerous far-right armed accelerationist groups, including members or groups affiliated with The Base, Atomwaffen, and the more loosely-organized boogaloo movement. Nevertheless, we must not mistake law enforcement repression as signaling an unequivocal antagonism between police and the far right or any degree of common cause between these targeted far-right groups and militant and revolutionary leftist movements.

4. The particularity of the three way fight is dependent on concrete social relations. Far-right and fascist groups draw on and respond differently to different social contexts. For example, during the interwar period, fascist movements drew from the imperialist aspirations of European nationalisms. In North America, far-right movements emerge in relation to broader ideological and material forms of settler colonialism (which includes—meaning that capital accumulation is imbricated in—elements of white supremacy, heteropatriarchy, ableism, and Indigenous dispossession).[18]
In North America, the historical development of liberal political and cultural institutions is inseparable from the development

of settler colonialism. Nonetheless, it would be undialectical to treat them uncritically as the same thing. Instead, in my view, it is more precise to contend that settler-state hegemony is formed by the mediation of bourgeois liberalism and white supremacist settlerism. I would define white supremacist settlerism as an ideological framework which privileges both white entitlement to land (possession or dominion) over the right of the colonized to sovereignty and autonomy, and entitlements encapsulated in what Du Bois calls the "public and psychological wage of whiteness." Examining the end of the Reconstruction period in the United States South after the Civil War, Du Bois argues that the potential for the formation of abolition democracy, built on solidarity between the Black and white proletariat, was defeated by the reorganization of settler-state hegemony along lines that ensured forms of deference and the institutionalization of racial control, as well as opening institutional access to education and social mobility to poor whites, drawing them, even if only aspirationally, into the petty bourgeoisie and labor aristocracy.[19]

Du Bois's analysis remains the prototype—though it must be theoretically corrected by incorporating the role that the settlement of the western frontier played in this dynamic—for conceptualizing settler-state hegemony and the role that whiteness plays within it. The presidential campaigns of 2020, in the midst of the COVID-19 pandemic and then the widespread anti-police uprising, offered two competing visions of reorganizing American settler-state hegemony—one which attempted to pull some system-oppositional far-right movements toward system-loyal organizing (embodied in the fall of 2020 as vigilantism) and the other which took on a form of superficial antifascism. But they also demonstrated that a common interest in defending settler-state hegemony against challenges from the revolutionary left and the liberation struggles of oppressed peoples forms the basis of the line of adjacency between bourgeois liberalism and white supremacist settlerism.

5. Far-right movements are system-loyal when they perceive that the entitlements of white supremacy can be advanced within bourgeois-democratic institutions, and they become insurgent when they perceive that these entitlements cannot.

In the first thesis, I stated that fascist groups appeal to an authoritarian vision of collective rebirth. In North American settler-colonial societies, far-right and fascist groups demand the re-entrenchment of the social and economic hierarchies that have enabled white social and economic mobility; they perceive that their social standing is in jeopardy and demand that settler-state hegemony be tilted "back" toward their advantage. In sum, far-right movements assert supposed "rights" of white settlerism which supersede the formal guarantees and protections granted through the liberal institutions of settler-state hegemony.

This thesis seemingly contradicts Lyons's definition of the contemporary far right offered in Thesis 2. Though contemporary far-right movements are system-oppositional today, this has not unequivocally been the case historically. Ker Lawrence, in "The Ku Klux Klan and Fascism" (1982), outlines how the KKK shifted between system-loyal and system-oppositional forms: in its earliest incarnation, the KKK was a "restorationist movement of the Confederacy"; in the 1920s it was a mainstream bourgeois nativist movement; in the 1960s it was a reactionary movement fighting to preserve segregation; then finally, around the time Lawrence was writing, it shifted to its present system-oppositional, insurgent position.[20]

I would suggest—as a provisional hypothesis which remains to be developed in more detail elsewhere—that liberalism and white settlerism were historically able to coexist in North America because the latter's interests did not substantially interfere with those of the former. Fascism failed to emerge as a profound challenge to American political hegemony in the 1930s and 1940s because, as Sakai notes, "white settler colonialism and fascism occupy the same ecological niche. Having one, capitalist society didn't yet need the other."[21] From the 1950s to the 1970s, a variety of civil rights struggles and liberation movements leveled a profound challenge to settler-state hegemony. Liberalism accommodated challenges from social justice movements by extending formal legal protections to marginalized groups and by introducing new patterns of economic redistribution (social welfare). This did not overturn the expectations and entitlements of the wages of whiteness. As Cheryl Harris contends, "after legalized segregation was overturned, whiteness as property evolved into a more modern form through the law's ratification of the settled expectations of relative white privilege as a legitimate and natural baseline."[22] In other words, white entitlements could be codified into law as long as they could be framed in ostensibly colorblind terms—and furthermore, these colorblind terms would contribute to the (incorrect) perception that systemic white supremacy had been pushed to the margins of American society.

As recent events reveal, settler-state hegemony is not immune to crisis. As Marx and Engels argue in *The Communist Manifesto*, the social position of the petty bourgeoisie is always tenuous because "their diminutive capital does not suffice for the scale on which Modern Industry is carried on." While the white petty bourgeoisie has repeatedly been "bought off" by social mobility or access to land (available due to Indigenous dispossession), even during the period of neoliberal austerity, that does not mean that settler-state hegemony will continue to organize future hegemonic blocs successfully. The threat remains that an insurgent fascist movement, organized around the rebirth of the settler-colonial project, will fill that hegemonic vacuum.

6. A revolutionary horizon is a necessary component to antifascist organizing; that is, there is no meaningful way in which fascism can be permanently defeated without overthrowing the conditions which give rise to it: capitalism and white supremacy and, in North America, settler-colonialism.

Militant antifascism is organized in order to meet the imminent threat of fascist organizing; it is an instantiation of community self-defense. A united front is necessary in situations where the revolutionary left is present but lacks a mass base, but it is always caught in a contradiction: the major left ideological currents—socialism, anarchism, and communism—converge in a united front but diverge around the particulars of the revolutionary horizon. While combatting fascism is the immediate task of militant antifascism, antifascists must maintain a revolutionary horizon, even if only in broad outline, in order to avoid being absorbed within the ideological parameters of liberal antifascism. At the same time, militants must also recognize that antifascist work cannot merely be absorbed into revolutionary work; antifascism is community self-defense.

7. Militant antifascism must uphold a diversity of tactics.

From a practical perspective, militant antifascism is distinguished from liberal antifascism by a willingness to use a diversity of tactics, up to and including physical confrontation, to disrupt far-right organizing. Effective militant organizing, though, must not transform the diversity of tactics into *merely* physical confrontation.[23] Antifascism seeks to raise the cost of fascist organizing, and that is the most obvious reason why a diversity of tactics plays an important role in organizing. As Robert F. Williams observed in 1962, racists "are most vicious and violent when they can practice violence with impunity."[24] Physical confrontation raises the stakes of fascist attempts to harass and intimidate communities as they organize. But it is important to emphasize that, in practice, physical confrontation still tends to come late: antifascists conduct research and publicize the fascist threat and dox fascists, we put pressure on supposedly community-accountable institutions to de-platform or no-platform far-right groups, when fascists rally we meet them in the streets to disrupt their actions. Militants uphold the importance of a diversity of tactics but, popular conceptions notwithstanding, that doesn't necessarily mean violence. The critical question is always: which tactic can cause the greatest disruption to far-right movements at each stage of organizing?

❦

Events of the last year especially have revealed the weaknesses of liberal mechanisms to stem far-right organizing. For years, liberal antifascists interpreted the lack of law enforcement pressure against the far right as a lack of urgent threat, and when the potential scope of far-right violence erupted into popular consciousness on January 6, 2021, it was years too late. The failure of far-right and fascist groups to undermine the transition of government power was due not to police repression (in fact, there was a distinct absence of police repression on that particular day), but primarily to internal organizational weaknesses, which I would attribute in part to pressure brought to bear on these groups over the last five years by antifascist organizing.

When confronted with emerging far-right movements, and unlike liberal antifascists, militant antifascists act sooner so that we don't have to take greater risks later. Antifascists must maintain a revolutionary horizon but at the same time remain focused on the immediate threat of fascist organizing. A world where fascists can openly organize is worse than one where they cannot. Though the German and Italian fascisms were historically defeated in 1945, it will take a greater effort to defeat fascism once and for all. Part of that work must be done now by a united front of militant antifascists.

NOTES

1. George Dimitrov, *The Fascist Offensive and Unity of the Working Class* (Paris: Foreign Languages Press, 2020), 4. Don Hamerquist discusses in passing how anarchist definitions of fascism during this time were similar to Dimitrov's line. See Don Hamerquist, "Fascism and Anti-Fascism," in Hamerquist et al., *Confronting Fascism: Discussion Documents for a Militant Movement*, 2nd edition (Montreal: Kersplebedeb, 2017), 30.

2. The Black Panther Party, "Call for a United Front against Fascism," in Bill V. Mullen and Christopher Vials, eds., *The U.S. Antifascism Reader* (London: Verso, 2020), 269.

3. See Dimitrov, *The Fascist Offensive*, 6: "Fascism is able to attract the masses because it demagogically appeals to their most urgent needs and demands."

4. See Enzo Traverso, *The New Faces of Fascism: Populism and the Far Right* (London: Verso, 2019); Samir Gandesha, "Posthuman Fascism," *Los Angeles Review of Books*, August 22, 2020; Alberto Toscano "The Long Shadow of Racial Fascism," *Boston Review*, October 28, 2020.

5. See, for example, Mark Bray, *Antifa: The Anti-fascist Handbook* (New York: Melville House, 2017); Daniel Sonabend, *We Fight Fascists: The 43 Group and Their Forgotten Battle for Post-war Britain* (London: Verso, 2019); Hilary Moore and James Tracy, *No Fascist USA! The John Brown Anti-Klan Committee and Lessons for Today's Movements* (San Francisco: City Lights, 2020). Note that this list does not include anti-fascist approaches developed by groups that framed their struggle in terms of national liberation, though they are certainly worthy of study as well.

6. Given that JBAKC was part of a post–Weather Underground anti-imperialist tendency aligned with the New Afrikan liberation movement, it is more appropriate to clarify that some of JBAKC's actions had, according to Don Hamerquist, an ambivalent relationship to the state. There were, he writes, "embarrassing pleas for 'police protection' from the fascists by supposedly revolutionary anti-fascists," and an emphasis on "legalism." By contrast, he argues, "it's hard to underestimate how important it was when ARA developed a principled stance against any cooperation with the state under the cover of opposing fascists." See Hamerquist, *A Brilliant Red Thread: Revolutionary Writings*, ed. Luis Brennan (Montreal: Kersplebedeb, 2023), 165–67.

7. Bray, *Antifa*, 172.

8. See D.Z. Shaw, "From German Communist Antifascism to a Contemporary United Front," in T. Derbent, *The German Communist Resistance 1933–1945* (Paris: Foreign Languages Press, 2021), 8–9.

9. As Matthew N. Lyons, notes, "repression … can even come in the name of antifascism, as when the Roosevelt administration used the war against the Axis powers to justify strike-breaking and the mass imprisonment of Japanese Americans." See *Insurgent Supremacists: The U.S. Far Right's Challenge to State and Empire* (Montreal/Oakland: Kersplebedeb/PM Press, 2018), ix.

10. Dimitrov, *The Fascist Offensive*, 4.

11. Don Hamerquist, "Fascism and Anti-Fascism," in *Confronting Fascism*, 41.

12. T. Derbent, *The German Communist Resistance 1933–1945* (Paris: Foreign Languages Press, 2021), 99. Despite the repeated assertions by paternalistic liberals that fascism is a working-class movement, even liberal historians acknowledge that workers "were always proportionally fewer than their share in the population." See Robert O. Paxton, *The Anatomy of Fascism* (New York: Vintage, 2004), 50.

13. Lambert Strether, "The Class Composition of the Capitol Rioters (First Cut)," *Naked Capitalism*, January 18, 2021.

14. Hamerquist argues, for example, that fascist labor policy under the Nazis extended beyond "the genocidal aspect of continuing primitive accumulation that is part of 'normal' capitalist development … . The German policy was the genocidal obliteration of already developed sections of the European working classes and the deliberate disruption of the social reproduction of labor in those sectors—all in the interests of a racialist demand for 'living space'." "Fascism and Anti-Fascism," in *Confronting Fascism*, 43; Lyons, *Insurgent Supremacists*, 255.

15. Lyons, *Insurgent Supremacists*, ii.

16. Lyons, *Insurgent Supremacists*, 28.

17. Lyons, *Insurgent Supremacists*, ii.

18. In *Confronting Fascism*, Hamerquist and Sakai both criticize the assumption that fascism (even in North America) will continue to be necessarily white supremacist. Within the discussions of the three way fight, the meaning of non-white participation in far-right movements remains an open debate. In my view, we must both assess the degree of non-white participation while also providing an explanation as to why this participation remains at the present moment marginal (for most individuals within ostensibly white supremacist movements or as autonomous organizations) within the broader far-right milieu. That account is provided in these theses.

19. W.E.B. Du Bois, *Black Reconstruction in America: An Essay Toward a History of the Part Which Black Folk Played in the Attempt to Reconstruct Democracy in America, 1860–1880*, ed. Henry Louis Gates, Jr. (Oxford: Oxford University Press, 2007), 573–74.

20. Ken Lawrence, "The Ku Klux Klan and Fascism," *Urgent Tasks* 14 (Fall/Winter 1982): 12. Reprinted in Bill V. Mullen and Christopher Vials, eds., *The U.S. Anti-fascism Reader* (London: Verso, 2020).

21. Sakai, "The Shock of Recognition," in *Confronting Fascism*, 130.

22. Cheryl Harris, "Whiteness as Property," *Harvard Law Review* 106, no. 8 (June 1993): 1714.

23. Indeed, Tammy Kovich contends, in a point that applies both to the creation of a broader antifascist culture and to the use of a diversity of tactics, that "we cannot focus almost exclusively on physical activities and/or traditionally male-dominated spaces. It's important to have spaces, roles, and activities that account for the variety of diversity of social

life—for example considering things like ability and age." Nor should we perpetuate gender stereotypes in organizing community self-defense. See Tammy Kovich et al., *Anti-Fascism against Machismo* (Montreal: Kersplebedeb, 2023), 68.

24. Robert F. Williams, *Negroes with Guns* (Detroit: Wayne State University Press, 1998), 4.

2. Between System-Loyal Vigilantism and System-Oppositional Violence

SYSTEM-LOYALTY AND THE FAR-RIGHT REACTION
TO THE ANTI-POLICE UPRISING

In what follows, I will suggest that, in response to the anti-police uprising which followed the murder of George Floyd and spread across the United States after protestors torched the 3rd police precinct building in Minneapolis, the Trump administration has made a move to pull far-right movements within a system-loyal ambit of settler-state hegemony. As with any analysis that attempts to interpret events as they unfold and as they have only recently unfolded, some of these impressions will unfortunately be shaped by oftentimes uncritical media and conflicting social media accounts, which could distort our perception of the situation on the ground and muddy our critical reflections. To remedy this, at least in part, I have relied as much as possible on research that has a stronger critical methodology, a clear and explicit ideological orientation, and a shared political commitment toward fighting fascism. Nonetheless, I expect that some of the following claims will need to be criticized and revised as the processes I describe play out.

In *Philosophy of Antifascism*, I propose the following thesis (to which I've made a minor adjustment in order to bring it into

---

Originally published on the *Three Way Fight* website, October 25, 2020.

line with the present discussion) to explain the relationship between far-right movements and settler-state hegemony:

> Far-right movements are system-loyal when they per-
> ceive that the entitlements of white supremacy can be
> advanced within bourgeois or democratic institutions,
> and they become insurgent when they perceive that
> these entitlements cannot.[1]

In my view, settler-state hegemony is stabilized when it can balance — or is *perceived* to balance — the interests of the bourgeoisie
and white petty bourgeois settlers, whose system-loyalty rests on
their access to, as W.E.B. Du Bois puts it, the "public and psychological wage" of whiteness. In *Black Reconstruction*, Du Bois
provides a paradigmatic example of this process of building
hegemony and white settlerism. In his view, during the era of
Reconstruction, it was an open question as to how American
hegemony was to be realigned after being torn asunder in the
Civil War. Though some of his phrasing — such as his evocations
of the dictatorship of the proletariat during Reconstruction — is
hyperbolic, Du Bois describes a series of shifting alliances between the Northern bourgeoisie, the Southern planter class, the
white proletariat, and the Black proletariat.

In the midst of the crisis, factions of white Southerners,
such as the Ku Klux Klan, revolted against Reconstruction-
era governance and carried out campaigns of terror predomi-
nantly against Black communities. (Of course, as Kwando
Mbiassi Kinshasa shows in his book *Black Resistance to the Ku
Klux Klan in the Wake of Civil War*, these Black communities also
fought back.) These class conflicts were resolved, and system-
oppositional white supremacist groups were pulled back toward
system-loyalty, as hegemony coalesced around the public and
psychological wages of whiteness: forms of deference, institutional access (to education, for example), the institutionalization of racial social control ("the police were from their ranks,
and courts, dependent upon their votes, treated them with

such leniency as to encourage lawlessness"), and social mobility (drawing poor whites into the petty bourgeoisie and labor aristocracy).[2] Part of this hegemony was brokered through labor organizing, as Du Bois notes, and, as later critics have described, part was through the westward expansion of the United States, facilitated by laws such as the Homestead Act of 1862 or the Southern Homestead Act of 1866.

The present conjuncture of the COVID-19 pandemic and the anti-police uprising in the United States has created an unprecedented economic and political crisis. If Ruth Wilson Gilmore is correct that neoliberal hegemony coalesced in part around "the prison fix," then it is fitting that the greatest challenge to this hegemony arrives in the form of a broad social movement against policing.[3] On its face, the 2020 American election appears to be a choice between two forms of stabilizing the neoliberal order through so-called "law and order": one where police violence will beat social unrest down with the baton of so-called objective right or one that more explicitly relishes brutality and cruelty. However, I believe that if we apply the concept of the three way fight to the present hegemonic crisis we can discern another possibility: Trump's validation of far-right vigilantism could also point toward a recomposition of settler-state hegemony through, in part, pulling far-right system-oppositional currents toward system-loyalty.

In *Philosophy of Antifascism*, I apply the concept of the three way fight to situate militant antifascism against forms of setter-state hegemony in Canada and the United States, which, in my view, are constituted through the state mediation of the interests of capital and white supremacy. These interests tend to manifest in a dialectic that mediates between bourgeois liberalism and popular and/or paramilitary white settler mobilizations. By differentiating between bourgeois liberalism and white supremacy, I do not mean that liberalism excludes racism or that white supremacy refuses the terms of bourgeois liberalism. I differentiate between the two in order to highlight their self-ascribed ideological forms, which represent (at least) two tendencies within setter-state governance and hegemony.

In schematic terms, liberalism manages hegemony through appeals to popular legitimacy (realized through institutions of representative government), formal protections for individual rights and private property (objective right), and repressive force (typically cast as rule of law). It manages challenges from the left by meeting demands for social justice in terms of formal equality, legal protection, and managing patterns of redistribution. It has pulled right-wing white settlerism within system-loyal parameters, at least since the 1960s if not before, by formalizing or ratifying various forms of oppression if these can be codified in colorblind terms. I am proposing that Trump's attempt to pull system-oppositional currents within the far right toward system-loyalty opens the possibility that settler-state hegemony could be recomposed through a more explicit nationalist white settlerism—though this is not a foregone conclusion. Indeed, his open appeals to vigilantism were not necessarily his first strategy. Trump's early messaging, which called on law enforcement to "dominate the streets," suggested that he initially thought anti-police demonstrations could be quickly contained.[4]

Nonetheless, Trump paved the way for a far-right reaction when he suggested that his administration would designate antifa as a "terrorist organization." Open street-level conflict between far-right and antifascist groups has been a persistent feature of the last four years, but this policy direction signaled that the balance of forces on the ground would be more sharply tilted against militant left-wing organizing. The reaction was almost immediate, as various far-right groups—parts of the Patriot movement (such as Oath Keepers), Proud Boys, boogaloo bois, and America First/Groyper factions—turned up at demonstrations.[5]

Media attention has typically focused on the violent character of the far-right reaction. It also tends to simplify the tensions and contradictions between state power and the far right. By contrast, through a comparison of how some of these far-right groups have fared over the course of the reaction, I will argue that we must distinguish between system-loyal vigilantism and system-oppositional violence. This requires, at the outset, defining our terms. In *Insurgent Supremacists*, Matthew N. Lyons defines the far right as those "political forces that (a) regard human inequality as natural, inevitable, or desirable and (b) reject the legitimacy of the established political system."[6] He opts for the category of "the far right" rather than "fascism" because the former is broader than the latter. This allows Lyons to investigate a wider range of right-wing social movements that would not typically be grouped under fascism; he is thereby able to establish points of contact, influence, and conflict between these groups. But more importantly, in Lyons's view, this approach captures right-wing groups that reject the legitimacy of the American political system. He concludes: "the resulting division between oppositional and system-loyal rightists is more significant than ideological differences about race, religion, economics, or other factors."[7] In my view, on the basis of the discussion of settler-state hegemony, far-right movements are oppositional insofar as they are anti-bourgeois or anti-liberal but nonetheless continue to accept or advocate for the "white settlerist" pillar of settler-state hegemony.

For our present purposes, I will define "system-oppositional" as a strategic orientation that is preparing for armed conflict with state power. Some groups—such as the Patriot movement—pursue a dual strategy, sometimes working within institutional structures of the American political system and sometimes opting for system-oppositional conflict (for example, in 2016 the Citizens for Constitutional Freedom, led by Ammon Bundy, occupied the Malheur National Wildlife Refuge for almost six weeks). Such groups can be pulled toward system-loyal avenues. As Lyons has recently written:

> If internet activism was the linchpin of Donald
> Trump's symbiotic relationship with the far right in
> 2016, physical violence and harassment play that role
> today. Whether they intimidate Black Lives Matter

protests or intensify them, far-right vigilantes drama-
tize Trump's claims that extraordinary measures are
needed to combat lawlessness. In return, his fearmon-
gering offers Patriot activists and other paramilitary
rightists validation, increased attention, and political
focus.[8]

I would currently classify the actions of the Proud Boys and
some factions of the Patriot movement as examples of system-
loyal vigilantism. We can expect, with system-loyal vigilantism,
relatively close affinities between police and, as one officer put
it, "heavily armed friendlies."[9] The close affinity between policing and system-loyal vigilantism is evident in many forms
across the United States, from Kenosha, Wisconsin—where officers validated the presence of armed individuals just before
Kyle Rittenhouse (a youth police cadet) shot three protesters,
killing two—to Portland, Oregon, where cops "stood by while
Proud Boys and militiamen, some brandishing guns, attacked
anti-fascist protesters; when the Proud Boys retreated, the cops
fired tear gas."[10]

But it is important to note that not all parts of the reaction
pursue system-loyal vigilantism. Right-wing accelerationist
groups, such as the "boogaloo bois," constitute a small niche
of reactionary system-opposition organized explicitly around
armed paramilitary capacity. The boogaloo bois are "a loose
collection of online insurrectionists, some of whom believe a
civil war with a tyrannical government is inevitable and in some
sense desirable."[11] They appeared almost immediately on the
scene of the anti-police demonstrations that followed the murder
of George Floyd. While anti-police organizers correctly identified the presence of boogaloo-style groups as antagonistic, these
groups have sometimes claimed that they support anti-police
demonstrations. For example, a widely circulated meme in boogaloo circles includes Eric Garner, Breonna Taylor, and Oscar
Grant, along with far-right militia martyrs such as Vicki and
Samuel Weaver, in a list of people killed by the police.[12]

From the perspective of the three way fight, this is a clear attempt at far-right entryism that failed. Furthermore, not all boogaloo movement actions were merely opportunistic in this sense; several attempted to use anti-police protests to sow armed conflict. In the month of June, two boogaloo movement members were charged with killing two law enforcement officers,[13] and seven others were arrested for weapons charges or plotting violent attacks.[14] In addition, according to data collected by Political Research Associates and the Institute for Research and Education on Human Rights, incidents between protesters and boogaloo groups spiked early and then quickly trailed off.[15] These two factors would suggest that law enforcement intervention sidelined the boogaloo movement's street-level protest capacity; however, as recent arrests show, law enforcement pressure has not yet incapacitated the movement's clandestine organizational capacities.[16]

TENTATIVE CONCLUSIONS

How do we assess the difference between system-loyal vigilantism and system-oppositional violence? And where does this distinction fit in the historical relationships between the militant left, the far right, and the police? Revolutionary and militant leftist movements challenge the social inequalities that law enforcement is tasked to protect, and law enforcement has long attacked leftist movements at both the organizational and ideological levels. By contrast, as both David Cunningham and Kristian Williams contend, law enforcement tends to focus on the violent actions committed by far-right movements. Cunningham, in his analysis of the FBI's COINTELPRO–White Hate operation in the 1960s, notes that the FBI focused on Klan groups, such as the United Klans of America, while ignoring the Citizens Councils, because (1) the latter's class position ensured system loyalty, and (2) the type of racist activities chosen by the Klan "refused to follow a tightly constrained path of acceptable resistance [and this] made it a threat to the good name of the anti-civil rights movement."[17] The FBI and the far-right groups targeted under COINTELPRO–White Hate, Cunningham argues, shared a cultural common ground (manifested in a defense of the segregationist status quo, patriotism, and anti-communism), but the latter became law enforcement targets when they plotted or carried out violent acts that threatened the status quo.

While the Klan in the 1960s was generally ideologically system-loyal, it is a basic premise of the three way fight that far-right groups are now typically system-oppositional. Despite this shift in far-right organizational characteristics, law enforcement follows a general pattern set in the 1960s: Williams notes that in the 1990s, "when the government pursued right-wing terrorists, its efforts tended to focus narrowly on prosecutable crimes, whereas investigations into environmentalists and anarchists during the same period sprawled broadly across the relevant movements and often took on an explicitly ideological tone."[18] Today, a similar pattern emerges. The Trump administration characterizes antifa as so-called "domestic terrorism." Though law enforcement curbs far-right movements organized around system-oppositional violence, there is a more general tolerance for system-loyal vigilantism. While Trump's attempt to pull some far-right groups toward a system-loyal position through explicitly validating vigilantism is a marked departure in contemporary American electoral politics, voting him out of office will not necessarily undermine the informal relationships forged through law enforcement and far-right opposition to militant leftist movements in the second half of 2020.

To conclude, I will examine a number of possible consequences of this return of vigilantism. Before November, it will remain unclear whether Trump's attempt to mobilize far-right vigilantism against the anti-police uprising marks the beginning of a recomposition of settler-state hegemony or whether it is an attempt to use vigilantism to shore up the neoliberal hegemony that is currently in crisis. In other words, it is unclear whether what we are witnessing involves the recomposition of hegemony around white settlerism, where white vigilantism remains a permanent feature of informal social control, or whether Trump will attempt to demobilize the far right after the election.

In the event of either a Trump victory and demobilization or a Biden victory (where Trump accepts the results), we can expect far-right movements presently mobilized to return to a system-oppositional stance. (For those skeptical of the scenario in which Trump demobilizes his far-right support, it is important to note that Trump did not ascend to political power on the basis of a mass movement, and so a potentially mass movement—with the attendant uncertainty and volatility that these movements bring—could play in his favor but could also create the opportunity for a far-right opposition beyond his control.)

If Trump remains in power through the continued mobilization of far-right vigilantism, these social forces could become de facto features of social control, fortifying repressive state violence while undermining liberal institutions and legal protections for women and minorities. We might also expect policies that materially cement such political alliances, e.g., the privatization of federal land holdings in areas where the Patriot movement has local presence. The possibility of reconstituting settler-state hegemony around a more explicit far-right white settlerism presents a much more dangerous terrain for antifascist and leftist organizing than the previous four years.

NOTES

1. D.Z. Shaw, *Philosophy of Antifascism: Punching Nazis and Fighting White Supremacy* (London: Rowman and Littlefield International, 2020), 178.

2. W.E.B. Du Bois, *Black Reconstruction in America: An Essay Toward a History of the Part Which Black Folk Played in the*

Attempt to Reconstruct Democracy in America, 1860–1880, ed. Henry Louis Gates, Jr. (Oxford: Oxford University Press, 2007), 573–74.

3. Ruth Wilson Gilmore, *Golden Gulag: Prisons, Surplus, Crisis, and Opposition in Globalizing California* (Berkeley: University of California Press, 2007), 87–127.

4. Katherine Faulders, Justin Fishel, and Alexander Mallin, "Trump, Barr Tell Governors to 'Dominate' Streets in Response to Unrest," abcnews, June 1, 2020.

5. Political Research Associates, "Police, Paramilitaries, and Protests for Racial Justice," Political Research Associates (website), June 3, 2020.

6. Matthew N. Lyons, *Insurgent Supremacists: The U.S. Far Right's Challenge to State and Empire* (Montreal/Oakland: Kersplebedeb/PM Press, 2018), ii.

7. Lyons, *Insurgent Supremacists*, ii.

8. Matthew N. Lyons, "Trump, the Far Right, and the Return of Vigilante Repression," *Three Way Fight* (website), September 1, 2020.

9. Kristian Williams, "U.S. Cops Are Treating White Militias as 'Heavily Armed Friendlies'," Truthout (website), September 17, 2020.

10. Williams, "U.S. Cops."

11. Political Research Associates, "Police, Paramilitaries, and Protests."

12. Robert Evans, "The Boogaloo Movement Is Not What You Think," bellingcat (website), May 27, 2020.

13. Richard Winton, Maura Dolan, and Anita Chabria, "Far-right 'Boogaloo Boys' Linked to Killing of California Law Officers and Other Violence," *Los Angeles Times*, June 17, 2020.

14. Cassie Miller, "The 'Boogaloo' Started as a Racist Meme," SPLC, June 5, 2020.

15. Political Research Associates, "Mapping Paramiltary and Far-Right Threats to Racial Justice," Political Research Associates (website), June 19, 2020.

16. Robert Snell and Melissa Nann Burke, "Plans to Kidnap Whitmer, Overthrow Government Spoiled, Officials Say," *The Detroit News*, October 8, 2020.

17. David Cunningham, *There's Something Happening Here: The New Left, the Klan, and FBI Counterintelligence* (University of California Press, 2005), 122.

18. Williams, "U.S. Cops."

3. Notes for a Critique of Dimitrov, the Orthodox Line on Fascism, and the Popular Front Strategy

I. THE THREE WAY FIGHT AND THE CRITIQUE OF THE ORTHODOX LINE

The three way fight is a revolutionary anticapitalist approach to fighting fascism. It begins from the premise that the best-known communist definition of fascism — the "orthodox line," which categorizes fascism as the politics or policy of the most reactionary elements of the bourgeoisie — not only led to historical failures in the struggle against fascism, but also fails to accurately theorize and describe the threat posed by the far right in contemporary North American settler-colonial societies (the focus of my work) and elsewhere.

The three way fight position emerged as a minority tendency within the antifascist work of Anti-Racist Action in the late 1990s and early 2000s.[1] A core premise of the three way fight is that revolutionary antifascist organizing struggles on two fronts, against capitalism (and its attendant forms of liberalism) and the far right. In other words, one basic premise of the three way fight — which breaks with the orthodox line — is that far-right movements (of which fascism is one tendency) are not merely the shock troops of the most reactionary capitalists.[2]

Originally published in *Material* 1 (2023).

They may at points collaborate with the police or find common cause with some factions of capital, but far-right movements are system-oppositional forms of organizing. What that means will be discussed in more detail below.

I assume, given that the three way fight position was, and is, a minority tendency within antifascist organizing, that the reader may not be entirely familiar with its history. The Three Way Fight project launched in 2004 as a non-sectarian forum for revolutionary anticapitalists to discuss and debate antifascist theory and politics. Although the Three Way Fight project began in 2004, the contributors and organizers associated with it have among them substantial experience in antifascist organizing. Don Hamerquist in particular has a history with the Sojourner Truth Organization (STO), the John Brown Anti-Klan Committee, and Anti-Racist Action.[3] While the work is driven by experience in antifascist organizing, contributors often refer back to a number of pivotal works that have developed the position: Hamerquist's and J. Sakai's essays in *Confronting Fascism* (2002), the anthology *My Enemy's Enemy* (2001), and, more recently, Matthew N. Lyons's *Insurgent Supremacists: The U.S. Far-Right's Challenge to State and Empire* (2018).[4]

My current research focuses on using the theoretical framework of the three way fight to rethink the history of revolutionary anticapitalist antifascism. The history of revolutionary critiques of fascism is often told from a European perspective because fascist movements first and most famously seized power in Italy and Germany. However, it remains insufficient to mechanically apply those critiques to a different socio-political conjuncture. Thus, I believe certain historical resources, which were not necessarily framed as "antifascist" at the time, open an alternative path to understanding fascism and the far right, especially the work of W.E.B. Du Bois and his concept of a "public and psychological wage" of whiteness, which has become better known — via David Roediger — as the "wages of whiteness."[5]

I will argue that there is a fundamental incompatibility, an epistemic rupture, and hence a split, between the orthodox line upheld by the Communist International (Comintern) and later the Black Panther Party, and an antifascist theory grounded in Du Bois's concept of the wages of whiteness. While it is a historical coincidence that Dimitrov's *The Fascist Offensive* and Du Bois's *Black Reconstruction* were both published in the same year, 1935, we cannot ignore that they were shaped by the challenges of the same historical moment—likewise with the fact that in the late 1960s, in the midst of a wave of reaction against Black liberation, the Panthers and James Boggs arrived at opposing theories of fascism, calling back to Dimitrov and Du Bois, respectively. In sum, Dimitrov and Du Bois represent two incompatible explanatory models for understanding fascism. Their "split," as it were, "haunts" the left in its struggle against capitalism and the far right up through the present day.

In this essay I have opted to focus on one particular aspect of the project: to submit both the orthodox line on fascism and the Popular Front strategy to a critique based on the three way fight position. Then, in the epilogue, I will sketch an alternative approach, taking Lenin's concept of the labor aristocracy and Du Bois's concept of the wages of whiteness as my points of departure. Thus, when I argue that there is an epistemological rupture between the orthodox line and the revolutionary antifascist trajectory that has informed the three way fight position, there is actually a dialectic of continuity and rupture. There is continuity in that the orthodox line and the three way fight both call back to anti-imperialism. Nevertheless, Du Bois's anti-imperialism and anti-racism—which, in my view, play an important intellectual role in the revolutionary antifascist alternative represented in the three way fight—do not merely amend, elaborate, or readjust the orthodox line. Between Dimitrov and Du Bois there is an epistemic rupture that must be acknowledged and theorized in order to advance the development of revolutionary, militant antifascist theory.

THE CLASS CHARACTER OF FASCISM AND ITS THREAT

The orthodox conception holds that fascism is *commanded* by the most reactionary elements of finance capital; in other words, the relationship between a fascist movement's organizational leadership, located in a narrow section of the bourgeoisie, and its mass base is top down. Rather that assert that fascism possesses an unequivocal class character, the three way fight position explores how the "mass" or "popular" elements of far-right movements recruit across class (and sometimes racial) lines.[6] In my view, in contemporary North America, they typically recruit among the petty bourgeoisie and the "worker elite" or "labor aristocracy" (including declassed or lumpen elements from these strata), who tend to shape the ideological contours and organizational direction of these movements. Therefore, the three way fight perspective maintains that there is a degree of relative autonomy—rather than the unilateral direction of command—between reactionary far-right ideologues amongst the bourgeoisie and far-right movements on the ground. The fact that there is relative autonomy between these groups does not preclude politicians, intellectuals, or military personnel from participating in, or providing leadership and legitimacy to, fascist social movements. However, this fact does mean that fascist movements cannot be treated as a mere *epiphenomenon* of capitalist rule. Instead, fascist movements are "system-oppositional," meaning they pose a social and political challenge to the status quo.

Therefore, the three way fight position describes fascism as a social movement involving a relatively autonomous and insurgent (potentially) mass base, which, like other far-right movements, challenges state power even though it promotes and aims to re-entrench economic and social hierarchies. On this basis, the three way fight situates militant antifascist struggle as a fight on two fronts, against two relatively autonomous social forces: against the far right (of which fascism is a part) and against bourgeois capitalist rule.

Here are three examples of three way fight discussions of fascism.

▶ In "Fascism and Anti-Fascism" (2002), Don Hamerquist observes "that *fascism has the potential to become a mass movement* with a substantial and genuine element of revolutionary anti-capitalism. Nothing but mistakes will result from treating it as 'bad' capitalism — as, in the language of the Comintern, 'the policy of the most reactionary sections of big capital' ... . The real danger presented by the emerging fascist movements and organizations is that they might gain a mass following among potentially insurgent workers and declassed strata through an historic default of the left." (my emphasis)[7]

▶ In "Two Ways of Looking at Fascism" (2008), Matthew N. Lyons proposes the following definition: "Fascism is a revolutionary form of right-wing populism, inspired by a totalitarian vision of collective rebirth, that challenges capitalist political and cultural power while promoting economic and social hierarchy."[8]

▶ In my work, I propose that "Fascism is a social movement involving a relatively autonomous and insurgent (potentially) mass base, driven by an authoritarian vision of collective rebirth, that challenges bourgeois institutional and cultural power, while re-entrenching economic and social hierarchies."

There are differences between us of emphasis and differences concerning which aspect of bourgeois or capitalist power far-right system-oppositional movements challenge. However, we share the following three convictions. First, that far-right street movements possess a degree of autonomy from far-right factions that may exist in institutions of power. Second, that the far right challenges some aspects of bourgeois institutional and cultural power. And, third, that fascism could be supported by some factions of capitalists, but that these factions do not command far-right movements, and that transclass collaboration would impose conditions on these reactionary factions of the bourgeoisie. In sum, underlying all three formulations is the concept that fascist social movements are not merely the shock troops of a reactionary faction of the bourgeoisie; they have a relative degree of autonomy and may even disrupt the ordinary functioning of bourgeois governance, even though they desire to re-entrench economic and social hierarchies within society.

Hence, it should be clear that the orthodox line, that "fascism in power is the open terrorist dictatorship of the most reactionary, most chauvinistic and most imperialist elements of finance capital,"[9] misses the mark. Despite its insufficiency, however, it remains the prevalent view within the left. For some, its appeal rests on its seeming conformity with Lenin's theory of imperialism. Lenin argues that politically, "imperialism is … a striving towards violence and reaction," while economically, it is marked by the predominance of finance capital over industrial capital.[10] For others, the orthodox line remains valuable as the underpinning for leftist coalition-building through popular fronts. The orthodox line characterizes fascism as the political tendency of a very narrow faction of finance capital, which permits revolutionary, militant, or vanguard formations to ally with non-revolutionary, generally liberal, organizations. For example, Dimitrov mentions "joint action with Social-Democratic Parties, reformist trade unions and other organizations of the toilers against the class enemies of the proletariat."[11]

A popular front can be a useful organizing tool for counter-mobilizing against far-right movements when they take to the streets. I will argue that Dimitrov's position, as a totality, directs popular fronts to build coalitions to pressure parliamentary systems to prevent them from preparing the path toward a fascist seizure of power. After discussing Dimitrov's Popular Front strategy, I will then briefly review the Black Panther Party's United Front Against Fascism. There, I will contend that the BPP's own antifascist attempt to mobilize a popular front to challenge the use of police violence was hemmed in by an unexamined assumption of legalism.

In brief, I will argue that this type of popular front strategy makes two mistakes. First, it risks mistaking intensified state repression, part of the ordinary functioning of capitalist power, for fascism. In other words, from a popular front perspective following the orthodox line, fascism is seen as an instrument of the most reactionary elements of capital, and the primary threat of fascism in power is that it implements a form of state power that is more repressive and reactionary than the ordinary functioning of capitalist power. Then, on the basis of this conception of fascism, popular front strategies tend toward pressuring the state apparatus to either forestall implementing the "preparatory stages" toward fascism or to revert to the ordinary functioning of bourgeois governance. In my view, organizing popular fronts to pressure parliamentary institutions is a rearguard strategy. Antifascist work must proactively focus on undermining the potentially mass or popular base of fascist organizing, such as no-platforming or community self-defense actions (which is how I refer to antifascist work to prevent fascist movements from claiming and holding public spaces).

SOCIAL DEMAGOGUERY AND THE
POTENTIAL MASS APPEAL OF FASCISM

Nevertheless, one could argue that Dimitrov explains the transclass character of fascism as a product of social demagoguery. In other words, he not only acknowledges the transclass character of fascism but also explains it as the product of propaganda that appeals to the needs and the demands, even a sense of economic justice, felt by the masses—promises that fascism's imperialist program cannot fulfill.

However, the three way fight rejects the top-down model of political action that is advanced by Dimitrov and that is emblematic of the communist theory of that period. He posits that fascism must be directed by some faction of capitalists that commands the mass base. In my view, pointing to social demagoguery is a superficial explanation that largely evades a materialist explanation of *why* fascist movements can appeal to a mass base. Hamerquist notes that orthodox communist analyses of fascism tend to credit the appeal of fascism to forms of false consciousness or temporary and accidental features of capitalist development; in sum, "there was little serious examination of the actual and potential mass popular appeal of fascism."[12] Indeed, I will argue that Dimitrov's explanation also sidesteps the racist and antisemitic underpinnings of fascist nationalism.

The three way fight position holds that fascist ideology is motivated by a totalizing vision of collective rebirth. Matthew N. Lyons arrived at this position (which I share) in "Two Ways of Looking at Fascism," in an attempt to synthesize Hamerquist's and Sakai's discussions of the system-oppositional character of fascism with the critique of fascist ideology carried out by liberal historian Roger Griffin. Griffin argues that fascist ideology is a populist "palingenetic" ultranationalism.[13] Since we have defined fascism as an insurgent, potentially mass movement, we need not adopt his characterization of fascist ideology as populist. For Lyons, fascism centers a myth of collective rebirth after a period of—or *the perception of*—crisis, decline, or decadence. The fascist defines the nation as the realization of an organic unity organized around what its protagonists see as a natural order. As Lyons summarizes, fascist ultranationalism "fundamentally rejects the liberal principles of pluralism and individual rights, as well as the socialist principles of class-based solidarity and internationalism, all of which threaten the nation's organic unity."[14] On this basis, I will critique Dimitrov's discussion of social demagoguery. I will also argue that far-right movements in North America have a very specific vision of national rebirth, one which views collective rebirth as the re-entrenchment of the social and political hierarchies of settler-state hegemony, but on terms conducive to these movements.

II. CRITIQUE OF THE ORTHODOX LINE

OVERVIEW

The orthodox communist line on fascism was put forward in 1933 by the Thirteenth Plenum of the Executive Committee of the Comintern. Two years later, it was implemented as the basis of the Popular Front line, which was announced and outlined by Georgi Dimitrov in two speeches to the Seventh Congress of the Communist International that were published not long thereafter: *The Fascist Offensive and the Tasks of the Communist International in the Fight for the Unity of the Working Class Against Fascism* as well as a separate speech, *Unity of the Working Class Against Fascism*.

Before outlining the critique of the orthodox line, I think it worthwhile to pause and consider how it came to have an enduring appeal. The Comintern's Popular Front line has been denounced at several junctures as "right opportunism," or attacked for sacrificing the political needs of local antifascist struggles to defend the Soviet Union. However, acknowledging these criticisms gets us no closer to understanding why the orthodox line has survived far beyond its application to the Popular Front line, pulled from Dimitrov's argument and re-elaborated within contemporary conjunctures.

One answer has to do with the format of Dimitrov's *The Fascist Offensive*: its textual organization is conducive to study and reference. Though almost three-quarters of the essay outlines now-obsolete instructions on organizing Popular Fronts, the first section, "Fascism and the Working Class," presents a concise synopsis of the problem, in which Dimitrov defines fascism and the political threat it represents to the proletariat, explains the transclass character of fascism's mass base as a product of social demagoguery, and, finally, forecasts the ultimate failure of fascism due to the primary contradiction of its class character. In large part, our analysis below focuses on a critical assessment of Dimitrov's well-known slogans and assertions from that section.

Then there are political answers to the question. On the

one hand, some adherents to the orthodox line are committed to defending and preserving an antifascist approach that has the imprimatur of "official" communism, and Dimitrov's essays, written as they were by the head of the Comintern, are as "official" as it gets. On the other hand, for some, the popular front is idealized as mass organizing that averts the sectarianism that plagues other types of communist organizing. These answers do not explain how the popular front line escaped the perimeters of communist and social-democratic organizing circles.

In his recent book, *Everything is Possible: Antifascism and the Left in the Age of Fascism*, Joseph Fronczak argues that it was antifascist organizing during 1934–1936 that forged the idea of "the left" as a "mass global collectivity" which transcends parties and national borders. In his view, popular front organizing (which included the Comintern's Popular Front work but was not led by it) played an important role in creating this new idea of the left.[15] In *Haunted by Hitler: Liberals, the Left, and the Fight against Fascism in the United States* (2014), Christopher Vials contends that antifascist cultural work, including aspects of the Popular Front in the 1930s and early 1940s, played a role in fortifying labor movements and antiracist struggles while creating "a remarkably tenacious political grammar that would help place the hard right on the defensive for a generation."[16] In my view, though, the Black Panther Party's United Front Against Fascism (UFAF) initiative is the most influential factor that explains the enduring appeal of the orthodox line and the popular front today. As Vials observes,

> the Panthers evoked fascism more often than any postwar political organization in the United States as a whole … . The BPP did not single-handedly add fascism to the lexicon of radicals in the late 1960s, but, as a result of their efforts, antifascism became a more conscious political mode among other politically emergent groups, particularly Latinos, Asian Americans, and white student radicals.[17]

Their "Call for a United Front against Fascism," announcing the UFAF conference (held in Oakland in July 1969), draws on Dimitrov's Popular Front essays. Their definition of fascism introduces a slight change that emphasizes the racist character of this capitalist reaction:

> Dimitrov: "fascism in power is the open terrorist dictatorship of the most reactionary, most chauvinistic and most imperialist elements of finance capital."[18]

> The Black Panther Party: "Fascism is the open terroristic dictatorship of the most reactionary, most chauvinistic (racist) and the most imperialist elements of finance capital."[19]

Immediately following the definition of fascism, the "Call" parallels, with some slight changes and deletions of historically dated references, Dimitrov's rejection of competing accounts of the class character of fascism.[20] On the basis of these parallels and due to the enormous political and cultural cachet that the BPP held at the end of the 1960s and early 1970s, the Panthers lent a renewed legitimacy to both the orthodox line and the popular front, which continues to the present day. Nevertheless, I will contend that their conscious appropriation of Dimitrov and the Popular Front implemented a legalist framework that defines fascism as the use of state violence which transgresses bourgeois legality, and antifascist work as coalition-building to counter fascism by pressuring state institutions to observe their supposed legal boundaries.

1. THE POPULAR FRONT:
ISOLATING FASCISM AND ITS THREAT

DIMITROV ON FASCISM IN POWER

Dimitrov describes the threat posed by fascism plainly in the opening paragraphs of *The Fascist Offensive*: the bourgeoisie needs fascism "to place the *whole* burden of crisis on the backs of the toilers," "to solve the problem of markets by enslaving the weak nations" through colonial annexation or repartition, and to smash revolutionary movements that aim to overthrow capitalism.[21] When we review the historical record, there is no doubt that fascist movements in Germany and Italy sought to break the political power of organized labor, to build nationalist sentiment through imperialist expansion, and to smash revolutionary movements. And we know that fascists of all eras are not only willing to use violence to suppress their opponents but that they *venerate violence itself*.

However, when we review Dimitrov's outline of how fascists wield power, we encounter numerous contradictions—one is especially prominent in his discussion of fascist state power. He states that the fascist accession to power "is not an *ordinary succession* of one bourgeois government by another, but a *substitution* for one State form of class domination of the bourgeoisie—bourgeois democracy—of another form—open terrorist dictatorship."[22] This claim draws a clear line between ordinary bourgeois governance and fascist state power. Because fascist state power implements an open terrorist dictatorship that interrupts normal bourgeois government, the Popular Front line permits communist parties to ally with non-revolutionary organizations as an emergency measure to prevent fascists from acceding to power.

The clear line between ordinary bourgeois governance and fascist state power begins to dissolve when Dimitrov attempts to explain the distinction further, i.e., when he criticizes the Social Democratic leadership for capitulating to fascists. He suggests that fascism ascends to power in the midst of political crisis within different camps of the bourgeoisie, and "even within the fascist camp itself."[23] Due to this struggle, he claims, "before the establishment of a fascist dictatorship, bourgeois governments usually pass through a number of preliminary stages and institute a number of reactionary measures, which directly facilitate the accession to power of fascism."[24]

Dimitrov argues that fascism in power transforms state power, transgressing the ordinary succession and functioning of bourgeois governance, and that fascism ascends to power typically after crises in bourgeois governance have proceeded through a series of preparatory stages. When we review the historical record, there is evidence that fascism transforms state power with crises in bourgeois governance preparing the way. As support for the former claim, the Nazis were not merely a typical bourgeois conservative party and their political program clearly transgressed bourgeois legality. But, as support for the latter claim, it was a conservative party leader, Franz von Papen, who in the midst of crisis "deposed the legitimately elected government of the state (*Land*) of Prussia ... and prevailed upon President Hindenburg to use his emergency powers to install a new state administration headed by von Papen" in 1932, the year before Hitler was named chancellor.[25] Nonetheless, the problem remains that Dimitrov's account focuses almost exclusively on bourgeois factional struggles and parliamentarian maneuvering. It is true that fascist movements, when they seek power, seek to exploit factional struggles within the ruling class. However, we cannot leave out how fascism leverages its organizational strength through its street-level or mass base.

Hence a practical and organizational problem arises. Dimitrov issues the clear instruction that Popular Front formations must "fight the reactionary measures of the bourgeoisie and the growth of fascism at these preparatory stages" of bourgeois crisis.[26] However, by treating the "preparatory stages" as moments of parliamentarian factional struggle, Dimitrov directs Popular Fronts toward coalition-building within the broader left to put popular pressure on parliamentarian institutions, in order to forestall non-fascist governments from preparing the way for fascism. In my view, antifascist organizing must begin the fight long before fascist movements build a parliamentarian base. Fascist movements are, first, street-level, potentially mass movements that utilize violence to attack, harass, and/or intimidate their opponents. Therefore, fascist movements are to some degree system-oppositional, i.e., willing to transgress bourgeois legality or challenge bourgeois institutional or cultural power. These aspects are already evident, or these so-called "preparatory stages" are already prepared, when fascist movements enter parliamentarian institutions. The three way fight position offers a clearer line of demarcation between far-right *movements* and ordinary bourgeois conservative parties.

Then there remains a contradiction within Dimitrov's account of the continuity and rupture between ordinary bourgeois governance and fascism in power. Because he does not consider how the potentially mass-based, system-oppositional aspects of fascist movements constitute a rupture with ordinary bourgeois governance, it appears that fascism and ordinary rule are two alternative forms of bourgeois governance. As a result, the lack of a clear demarcation permits a conceptual confusion between the repressive features of ordinary bourgeois governance and fascism. For instance, in "Fascism: Some Common Misconceptions" (1978), Noel Ignatiev criticizes the broad application of the term "fascism," noting that welfare cuts, anti-union legislation, suppression of dissent, and increased police powers are all examples of ordinary bourgeois governance that have been "described as 'fascist,' or at the very least as steps toward fascism, by many left-wing organizations."[27]

THE UNITED FRONT AGAINST FASCISM

We may bring the underlying problem into sharper relief by examining the revival of the popular front line by the Black Panther Party in 1969, when it called the United Front Against Fascism conference in order to form a multiracial coalition to defend the BPP. Delegates to the conference were to set up local chapters of the National Committee to Combat Fascism. The "Call" for the UFAF conference states:

> Because of the rise in political awareness of Black people, the high degree of student activism and the overall expansion of progressive forces, this government is finding it necessary to drop its disguise of democracy and go openly into FASCISM.[28]

I have already identified several similarities between Dimitrov and the BPP's "Call," including the definition of fascism as the open terrorist dictatorship of the most reactionary elements of finance capital. The excerpted passage above additionally describes the counter-revolutionary character of fascism. Elsewhere, the Panthers also attempt to contrast fascism with the ordinary functioning of bourgeois rule, while maintaining the particularity of U.S. anti-Black racism. Kathleen Cleaver writes, in "Racism, Fascism, and Political Murder" (1968), that

> The advent of fascism in the United States is most clearly visible in the suppression of the black liberation struggle in the nationwide political imprisonment and assassination of black leaders, coupled with the concentration of massive police power in the ghettos of the black community across the country .... Black people have always been subjected to [a] police state and have moved to organize against it, but the structure is now moving to encompass the entire country.[29]

Cleaver's account recognizes that Black communities face suppression as part of the ordinary business of bourgeois rule, but she notes two new features of state violence: political assassination (among other forms of intensifying the suppression of the Black liberation struggle) and the expansion of police violence in order to suppress white dissent. Her position is largely recapitulated in the "Call" for the UFAF conference.

Surprisingly, then, the BPP sought to fight back through legal pressure. Vials notes that the Panthers had a "modest domestic legislative goal ... decentralized policing, wherein black and white neighborhoods would self-manage the police in their respective communities. In fact, a legally drawn petition for a referendum on community policing in the city of Oakland was already in place at the time of the conference."[30] Numerous critics have argued that the UFAF initiative marked a shift toward reformism. I'm not sure "reformism" best describes the political framework here, so I will instead explore how the Panthers inadvertently established a legalistic framework for antifascist work.

In *We Want Freedom*, his semi-autobiographical history of the Black Panther Party, Mumia Abu-Jamal argues that the underlying philosophical basis of the BPP's organizational efforts was legalism. He writes:

> While some might identify the philosophical basis [of the BPP] as Marxism, or its later variation, Maoism, others would prefer Black Nationalism, Black revolutionary internationalism, or, as we have suggested, Malcolmism.

> None of these truly answer the question, for while they identify a stage of the Party's ideological development, the underlying philosophical approach, as based in Huey [Newton] as the heart of the Party, was essentially a legalist one.[31]

We typically describe social movements that limit their activity to legal avenues as legalist. Here, Abu-Jamal uses the term to describe a theory of state power; thus, legalism is a belief "that there were limits to what the government would do to preserve its hold on power."[32] It has often been noted that Newton placed a significant value on legal concepts, but Abu-Jamal argues that legalism underlay much of the BPP's work. The Panthers' use of self-defense was couched in the assertion of constitutional rights, while core documents such as the 10-Point Platform and Program cite the U.S. Constitution and the Declaration of Independence.[33]

Abu-Jamal contends that, due to its unexamined legalist assumptions about state power, the Black Panther Party failed to anticipate the counterinsurgency measures that the U.S. security apparatus would take to undermine its organizing. Here, I want to apply Abu-Jamal's thesis to the BPP's antifascist work. In my view, Dimitrov's line (encompassing both the orthodox line and the Popular Front strategy) appeared theoretically viable because the BPP upheld an unexamined adherence to a legalist strategy. The "advent of fascism," in Cleaver's terms, occurs when police power oversteps the limits of bourgeois legality, which the United Front Against Fascism sought to combat through legal pressure. The Panthers were not alone in advocating for some degree of community control over policing. However, the BPP differed from groups such as the Deacons for Defense because they consciously adopted the mantle of a revolutionary vanguard party.

The BPP's antifascist work was torn by a contradiction between its explicit ideological development and its philosophical basis. Cleaver writes, for instance, in "Racism, Fascism, and Political Murder," that "the day when the state and its police power ceases to protect the community but in turn attacks the people of the community has arrived in this country. This is the first stage of building a total police state."[34] She may of course be evoking liberal rhetoric to interpolate the liberal-minded reader. Whether or not this is her intent, however, her argument assumes the liberal premise that the objective, universal basis of policing is community safety, rather than the repressive force required to maintain class (and racial) rule. Hence this underlying assumption contradicts the BPP's explicit ideological position, although it would fit within what Abu-Jamal refers to as its legalist philosophical basis. In sum, there is a contradiction between the BPP's philosophical basis and its ideological position, generally aligned with a Marxist position, that police are an instrument of class (and racial) rule. In *The Civil War in France*, Marx writes:

> At the same pace at which the progress of modern industry developed, widened, intensified the class antagonism between capital and labour, the state power assumed more and more the character of the national power of capital over labour, of a public force organized for social enslavement, of an engine of class despotism. After every revolution marking a progressive phase in the class struggle, the purely repressive character of the state power stands out in bolder and bolder relief.[35]

Obviously, Marx wrote before the historical emergence of fascism. Perhaps one could deduce, on the basis of Marx's observation, a theory of preparatory stages anticipating fascism. However, I would contend that his analysis of police power and the state in *The Civil War in France* supports the contention that the intensification of repressive measures to attack revolutionary movements may occur as part of the ordinary measures of bourgeois class rule. In other words, state repression in itself is not a sufficient condition to categorize a state as fascist.

It is my view that the theoretical and practical framework constituted by the combination of the orthodox line and the popular front strategy leads antifascist work to defend democratic and legalist, rather than militant, political goals, as many critics have shown. Robin D.G. Kelley, in *Hammer and Hoe*, observes that during the Popular Front period the CPUSA

> practically ceased to function as an independent, autonomous organization ... the failure of the CIO's Operation Dixie, anticommunism within the AFL-CIO, not to mention the anticommunism of the NAACP, weakened or destroyed the Communist-led unions,

leaving an indelible mark on the next wave of civil rights activists and possibly arresting what may have been a broader economic and social justice agenda.[36]

Given the ongoing political and cultural interest in the Black Panther Party, its antifascist work may have also left an indelible mark on the "common sense" view of what fascism is and how to fight it. However, ultimately, it is my view that Dimitrov's account of the Popular Front strategy and its underlying theoretical basis sets limiting parameters on antifascist work, parameters that too narrowly focus on preventing parliamentarian institutions from preparing the stage for the fascist seizure of power.[37]

2. THE CLASS CHARACTER OF FASCISM AND THE PROBLEM OF DEMAGOGUERY

Dimitrov defines fascism as a program of the most reactionary or extreme faction of the bourgeoisie, and yet, he must still explain one of the most glaring aspects of fascist movements: their mass base. Throughout *The Fascist Offensive*, Dimitrov explains the mass base and transclass character of fascist movements as a product of social demagoguery. Dimitrov is not the first to point toward social demagoguery to explain the mass, transclass base of fascism; by 1935 it had become a longstanding practice of the Comintern. For example, in 1922, the Fourth Congress's resolution "On the Tactics of the Comintern" included the statement that "the Fascists do not merely form narrow counter-revolutionary fighting organisations, armed to the teeth, but also attempt through social demagoguery to achieve a base among the masses."[38] However, social demagoguery is an insufficient explanation for the appeal of fascism. By contrast, Du Bois's concept of the wages of whiteness can explain the appeal through material interests and identity formation. The concept of the wages of whiteness provides content to the ideology of North American far-right movements, which seek to re-entrench social and economic hierarchies that benefit white settlers.

On the basis of the orthodox line, Dimitrov argues that fascism represents the narrow interests of a small section of reactionary imperialists. In order to appeal to a mass base, he contends, fascists use demagoguery to manipulate the attitudes and actions of other classes. He notes, correctly, that fascists adapt their rhetoric to the specific conditions of each country and even to the specific conditions of various social strata. Nonetheless, I would argue that Dimitrov presents the appeal of fascist rhetoric as superficial. In other words, there is an underlying assumption that if the demagogic content is dispelled the masses would then be available for communist organizing. In sum, Dimitrov does not examine the pull of available cultural or ideological materials—themselves grounded in historically specific material *conditions*—that make such rhetoric legible and persuasive.

Let us return to the text. Dimitrov contends that fascists gain a mass base by appealing to needs and demands unmet within bourgeois political systems and by crowding into the political terrain of the communists:

> Fascism is able to attract the masses because it demagogically appeals to their *most urgent needs and demands*. Fascism not only inflames prejudices that are deeply ingrained in the masses but also plays on the better sentiments of the masses, on their sense of justice, and sometimes even on their revolutionary traditions. Why do the German fascists, those lackeys of the big bourgeoisie and mortal enemies of Socialism, represent themselves to the masses as "Socialists," and depict their accession to power as a "revolution"? Because they try to exploit the faith in revolution, the urge towards Socialism, which lives in the hearts of the broad masses of the toilers of Germany.[39]

To summarize, he contends that fascists have gained a foothold amongst the masses because their promises meet the masses' desire for economic justice. He then argues that fascism is by necessity unstable — it cannot meet the promises it makes because it cannot overcome the class contradictions inherent in capitalist accumulation. Thus, the anticapitalist demagoguery of fascism is contradicted by its capitalist program.[40]

Dimitrov appears confident that the contradiction between fascist demagoguery and its economic basis will undo its grip on the masses. However, demagoguery, we should recall, is a form of political persuasion that appeals to the desires *and* the prejudices of its target audience. Therefore, the appeal or persuasiveness of fascist rhetoric cannot be evaluated on a solely economic basis. Dimitrov himself points to a countervailing aspect of fascist rhetoric that would displace merely economic criteria: nationalism.

> Fascism acts in the interests of the extreme imperialists, but it presents itself to the masses in the guise of champion of an ill-treated nation, and appeals to outraged national sentiments, as German fascism did, for instance, when it won the support of the masses by the slogan "Against the Versailles Treaty!"[41]

This passage epitomizes several problems with the Comintern's position on nationalism during this period. Torkil Lauesen argues that during the 1930s the Comintern revised its position on nationalism in the interest of defending the Soviet Union and in belated recognition that the working classes of the imperialist core had been won over by chauvinism and opportunism (a belated recognition, because communists from Lenin on had underestimated the size and strength of the labor aristocracy).[42] Thus, in the passage above, Dimitrov departs from Lenin's position on nationalism and imperialism. Lenin had argued that imperialism is characterized by competition between imperialist countries for colonial holdings. By contrast, Dimitrov suggests that nationalist sentiments within the imperial core may be salvaged for popular front work despite their historical formation through imperialism. There is, however, no discussion of how salvaging imperialist nationalisms affects oppressed nations within the imperialist core. In the U.S., the Popular Front strategy, which permitted a degree of nationalist sentiment among the white working classes, asserted the fight for equal status for Black Americans rather than self-determination in the Black Belt.[43] Then, near the conclusion of *The Fascist Offensive*, Dimitrov alleges that communism is opposed to both "bourgeois nationalism" and "national nihilism," and thus the principled opposition to bourgeois nationalism does not permit communists to "sneer at all the national sentiments of the broad toiling masses."[44] Here, the opposition of nationalism and "national nihilism" deflects from the actual opposition between nationalism and internationalism.

For our purposes, Dimitrov's superficial reference to nationalism precludes a dialectical interpretation of fascist rhetoric, which would synthesize the fascist appeals to both anticapitalist sentiments and nationalism. His work belies the assumption that the economic basis of fascism will ultimately dispel its demagogic promises, although he cautions that "fascism will not collapse automatically."[45] But fascists do not merely exploit the "faith in revolution" or the "urge towards Socialism" in the masses, as if they are crowding out the Communist Party. Instead, fascists assert an entirely different theory of social change grounded in a national rebirth—in Griffin's terms, "palingenetic ultranationalism."[46] Griffin argues that ultranationalism presents a concept of nationalism

> as a "higher" racial, historical, spiritual or organic reality ... . Such a community is regarded by its protagonists as a natural order which can be contaminated by miscegenation and immigration, by the anarchic, unpatriotic mentality encouraged by liberal individualism, internationalist socialism, and by any number of

"alien" forces allegedly unleashed by "modern" society, for example the rise of the "masses," the decay of moral values, the "levelling" of society, cosmopolitanism, feminism, and consumerism.[47]

Palingenetic ultranationalism also has a built-in explanation of its own failure: the natural order of the community is always under threat from external, alien forces. Within its own ideological parameters, each failure of the fascist program can be attributed to alien forces that block national rebirth. For example, the Nazis can mobilize antisemitic conspiracy theories to attack ruling "elites" rather than the bourgeoisie, or to attack communists ("Judeo-Bolshevism") for fomenting division, for undermining the supposed shared national interests between workers and the owners of the means of production.

In sum, Dimitrov's discussion of social demagoguery remains a superficial account of how fascism appeals to the prejudices of its potential mass base. His brief discussion of nationalism sidesteps issues of racism and antisemitism, sexism is broached only in a brief section on women's work, and he makes only passing mention of eugenics.[48] There is, in the Popular Front strategy, an unwillingness to deal with the motivating prejudices of the popular base for fascism. I have distinguished between fascist rhetoric and fascist social demagoguery in order to emphasize how Dimitrov fails to account for the motivating prejudices of fascist movements.

EPILOGUE: THE WAGES OF WHITENESS

In the second, most extensive section of *The Fascist Offensive*, handling Popular Front strategies, Dimitrov observes: "in contradistinction to German fascism, which acts under anti-constitutional slogans, American fascism tries to portray itself as the custodian of the constitution and 'American democracy'."[49]

He attributes the difference to American parochialism but does not explain its conditions or content or what this means.

The ideological differences between German fascism and American fascism are due to their different specific historical and political circumstances. American far-right movements could, and some still do, frame themselves as the true custodians of the Constitution and democracy because the United States is a settler-colonial state, which has integrated elements of bourgeois democratic parliamentarianism and elements of white supremacism into its social, political, and economic institutions. Commenting on the failure of American fascist movements to gain a mass base in the 1930s, Sakai contends that "white settler colonialism and fascism occupy the same ecological niche. Having one, capitalist society didn't yet need the other."[50] Settlerism and fascism are, in his view, two types of "popular oppressor cultures."

I define white settlerism as an ideological framework that privileges both white (male) entitlement to land (possession or dominion) over the right of the colonized to sovereignty and autonomy, and entitlements encapsulated in the wages of whiteness. When white settlerism or the social and political hierarchies entrenched in settler-colonial societies fall into crisis, or are perceived to have fallen into crisis, then far-right movements—which seek to re-entrench the political and social hierarchies of settler-state hegemony—gain traction. In what follows, I will briefly reconstruct the theoretical trajectory of this alternative revolutionary approach to understanding fascist and far-right movements.

As we have noted above, Dimitrov's characterization of fascism seemingly accords with Lenin's theory of imperialism, while nevertheless permitting a Popular Front strategy. In fact, Dimitrov's discussions of imperialism leave out one crucial aspect: the formation of the labor aristocracy within imperialist nations. The concept of the labor aristocracy captures how workers within the imperialist core receive a "wage" based on the superprofits expropriated from the workers of oppressed or colonial nations. Du Bois's analysis of the wages of white-ness is motivated by a similar concern. I cannot fully explore the parallels between Lenin and Du Bois here. However, I be-lieve that critics generally understand the compensation of the wages of whiteness or labor aristocracy to be "low," and hence not useful for understanding the social base of far-right and fas-cist movements. I believe this general understanding is incorrect, although it may have a partial basis in the writings of Lenin and Du Bois themselves.

For both Lenin and Du Bois, during the period of 1914–1916, the concept of the labor aristocracy contributes to under-standing how parts of the working class threw their support be-hind World War I. Lenin seeks to explain the economic grounds of social chauvinism and opportunism, and while Du Bois's concern is similar, he argues additionally in "The African Roots of War" (1915) that the economics of imperialism are a factor in the formation of whiteness.[51] What I want to highlight here is how Lenin characterizes the "bribe" required to pay off the labor aristocracy for supporting imperialism. Imperialism is de-fined in part by imperialist countries—the "Great Powers"—liv-ing at the expense of the colonies. The partition of the world is complete, however, which provokes imperial competition and ultimately war in order to repartition the colonial territories. In "Imperialism and the Split in Socialism" (1916), he writes:

> monopoly yields *superprofits*, i.e., a surplus of profits over and above the capitalist profits that are normal and customary all over the world. The capitalists *can* devote a part (and not a small one, at that!) of these superprofits to bribe *their own* workers, to create something like an alliance … between the workers of the given nation and their capitalists *against* the other countries … . And how this little sop is divided among the labour ministers, "labour representatives" (re-member Engels's splendid analysis of the term), labour members of war industries committees, labour officials,

workers belonging to the narrow craft unions, office employees, etc., etc., is a secondary question.[52]

Several of Lenin's key writings from this period give the impression that he considers the labor aristocracy to be a narrow stratum of workers who receive a small bribe in terms of wages and social or political access. There is some inconsistency in his characterization of the monetary portion of the bribe. In the passage above, he observes that the labor aristocracy receives "not a small" portion of superprofits, but elsewhere he refers to this narrow stratum of workers as getting "but *morsels* of the privileges of their 'own' national capital."[53] Lenin also contends that the bribe is temporary and unsustainable. Although the English labor aristocracy had been bribed for decades, he argues that it is "improbable, if not impossible," given the contemporary challenges to the monopoly of finance capital and the conflagration of imperialist war, for numerous imperialist countries to sustain their respective labor aristocracies.[54] Du Bois's "The African Roots of War" provides an interesting contrast. While Lenin sees a "moribund" and "already dying" capitalism on the precipice, Du Bois argues that the extraction of wealth from the colonies is only beginning: the exploitation of African workers "would furnish to their masters a spoil exceeding the gold-haunted dreams of the most modern of imperialists."[55]

In 1920, in "The Second Congress of the Communist International," Lenin continues to maintain that opportunism in imperialist countries is grounded economically in superprofits derived from the exploitation of oppressed peoples. However, while he had previously treated the labor aristocracy as a narrow stratum of the working class, in this text he avers that the economic returns of the exploitation of colonized and oppressed peoples affects the whole "culture of advanced countries."[56] He writes:

The whole thing boils down to nothing but bribery. It is done in a thousand different ways: by increasing cultural facilities in the largest centres, by creating educational institutions, and by providing co-operative, trade union and parliamentary leaders with thousands of cushy jobs.[57]

Despite the characterization of this transfer of wealth as "bribery," Lenin now suggests that the social and economic formation of the labor aristocracy has deeper economic roots than he had previously anticipated. During the period of 1914–16 the distribution of the wages of the labor aristocracy was treated as a "secondary question" that referred to points of political access and social status for a narrow, upper stratum of the working class. In 1920, he attempts to ground the labor aristocracy within broader European culture and in social and economic conditions, and he suggests that these "wages" buy more than mere political access or social status; they also provide cultural and educational opportunities to this worker elite. Nevertheless, these passages do not develop a full portrait of the social and political ramifications of the formation of a permanent labor aristocracy. The Communist International did not subsequently take up a theory of labor aristocracy as a task. Indeed, developing such a theory and applying it to fighting fascism was deliberately sidestepped by the Popular Front strategy.[58]

Du Bois's *Black Reconstruction* mentions fascism only in passing. However, his account of the wages of whiteness remains a model for understanding how the hegemony that circulates around whiteness is formed. In Chapter 16, "Back to Slavery," he argues that the struggle for abolition democracy, which followed Emancipation, was defeated by the formation of a white political identity that aligned the white working class with the white capitalist class. Summarizing the analysis of Chapter 16, which is more complex than I am able to present here, Du Bois writes:

It must be remembered that the white group of laborers, while they received a low wage, were compensated in part by a sort of public and psychological wage. They were given public deference and titles of courtesy because they were white. They were admitted freely with all classes of white people to public functions, public parks, and the best schools. The police were drawn from their ranks, and the courts, dependent upon their votes, treated them with such leniency as to encourage lawlessness. Their vote selected public officials, and while this had small effect upon the economic situation, it had great effect upon their personal treatment and the deference shown them. White schoolhouses were the best in the community, and conspicuously placed, and they cost anywhere from twice to ten times as much per capita as the colored schools.[59]

There are numerous clear parallels here between Du Bois and Lenin's analyses from 1920, when the latter mentions that part of the wage of the labor aristocracy includes access to education and cultural institutions. Some critics of Du Bois take this passage to imply that the wages of whiteness are low. However, I believe this particular observation at this point in *Black Reconstruction* is temporally bound to the *emergence* of a white labor aristocracy in the 1870s. In essays such as "Marxism and the Negro Problem," Du Bois addresses how a much wider gulf between white workers and Black workers subsequently emerged through developments in production and social-demographic change, which was then codified by disenfranchisement of the latter and the Color Bar.[60] Yet, Kevin Bruyneel identifies one way in which Du Bois does underestimate the wages of whiteness: by neglecting to situate Reconstruction in relation to the dispossession of Indigenous land and the white settlement of what is now the western United States, facilitated during the era of the Civil War and Reconstruction by the Homestead Act of 1862 and the General (or Dawes) Allotment Act of 1887. Bruyneel argues that, due to codified discrimination and violent intimidation against Black people through that period, white settlers claimed significant benefit from this and other Homestead Acts. This meant that access, or the prospect of access, to land *as* property was a "wage" conferred to whiteness as a socioeconomic benefit with vital political and social meaning during the late nineteenth-century consolidation of the racial and colonial capitalist system of the United States.[61]

Du Bois never quite brought settler-colonialism into focus, whether in *Black Reconstruction* or elsewhere; it remained a lacuna in his concept of the wages of whiteness. In the late 1960s, however, James Boggs—drawing on the work of Du Bois— linked the formation of the white worker elite to the failure of Reconstruction and the westward expansion of the U.S., while ultimately identifying this white worker elite as the "grass roots" base for fascism.[62] How Boggs's account of white settlerism and fascism places him at odds with the Black Panther Party's embrace of the orthodox line and the popular front strategy is an argument to be made another day.

❧ ❧ ❧

I have only sought to introduce and outline themes to a much larger and more complex work. We must begin critique somewhere in order to dispense with the certitudes and dogmas that surround the orthodox line on fascism. Once these are dispelled, we may begin to reconstruct the history of a critical, revolutionary antifascist theory that combats far-right movements within the context of North American settler-colonialism. I submit these notes in their incomplete and preliminary state for comradely criticism.

NOTES

1. See Shannon Clay et al., *We Go Where They Go: The Story of Anti-Racist Action* (Oakland: PM Press, 2023), 3: "First founded in 1987, Anti-Racist Action was a militant, direct-action-oriented, radical left political movement active in the United States and Canada."

2. Matthew N. Lyons defines the far right as inclusive of "political forces that (a) regard human inequality as natural, inevitable, or desirable and (b) reject the legitimacy of the established political system." See Lyons, *Insurgent Supremacists: The U.S. Far Right's Challenge to State and Empire* (Montreal/Oakland: Kersplebedeb/PM Press, 2018), ii. Throughout this essay, I will refer to the far right if I think it is important to suggest that a particular observation about fascist movements applies to the far right as a whole, otherwise I will refer to fascism (which I define below).

3. Hamerquist recounts his political background in *A Brilliant Red Thread: Revolutionary Writings from Don Hamerquist*, ed. Luis Brennan (Montreal: Kersplebedeb, 2023). For histories of these groups see, respectively: Michael Staudenmaier, *Truth and Revolution: A History of the Sojourner Truth Organization 1969–1986* (Oakland: AK Press, 2012); Hilary Moore and James Tracy, *No Fascist USA! The John Brown Anti-Klan Committee and Lessons for Today's Movements* (San Francisco: City Lights, 2020); and Clay et al., *We Go Where They Go.*

4. See also Xtn Alexander and Matthew N. Lyons, eds., *Three Way Fight: Revolutionary Politics and Antifascism* (Montreal/Oakland: Kersplebedeb/PM Press, 2024).

5. David R. Roediger, *The Wages of Whiteness: Race and the Making of the American Working Class*, revised edition (London: Verso, 1999).

6. Hamerquist describes this as the "transclass" character of fascism. I will also use this terminology at points. Regarding far-right recruitment across class and racial lines, see Lyons, *Insurgent Supremacists*.

7. Hamerquist, "Fascism and Anti-Fascism," in *Confronting Fascism: Discussion Documents for a Militant Movement*. 2nd edition (Montreal: Kersplebedeb, 2017), 28–29. In his contribution to *Confronting Fascism*, J. Sakai challenges Hamerquist's claim that far-right movements hold anti-capitalist bona fides; instead, he argues that far-right movements exploit and modulate sexist and settlerist social structures and ideologies already present in North American societies to build insurgent street-level movements. He notes that fascist movements are "anti-bourgeois but not anti-capitalist." See Sakai, "The Shock of Recognition," 122.

8. Matthew N. Lyons, *Insurgent Supremacists*, 253. "Two Ways of Looking at Fascism" is reproduced as an appendix to *Insurgent Supremacists*.

9. George Dimitrov, *The Fascist Offensive and Unity of the Working Class* (Paris: Foreign Languages Press, 2020), 4. In the FLP edition, text for the former essay is based on an edition produced by Modern Publishers of Sydney (1935), and the latter is based on one from Lawrence and Wishart (1938). (This information was provided in correspondence with one of the editors).

10. Lenin, *Imperialism, the Highest Stage of Capitalism* (Paris: Foreign Languages Press, 2020), 94.

11. Dimitrov, *The Fascist Offensive*, 28.

12. Hamerquist, "Fascism and Anti-Fascism," 31.

13. Roger Griffin, *The Nature of Fascism* (London: Pinter Publishers, 1991), 26. The term "palingenesis" is derived from

the Greek *palin* (again, anew) and *genesis* (creation, birth), to signify a sense or rebirth or regeneration.

14. Lyons, *Insurgent Supremacists*, 246.

15. Joseph Fronczak, *Everything is Possible: Antifascism and the Left in the Age of Fascism* (New Haven: Yale University Press, 2023).

16. Christopher Vials, *Haunted by Hitler* (Amherst: University of Massachusetts Press, 2014), 33.

17. Vials, *Haunted by Hitler*, 160–61.

18. George Dimitrov, *The Fascist Offensive*, 4.

19. Black Panther Party, "Call for a United Front against Fascism," in *The U.S. Antifascism Reader*, ed. Bill V. Mullen and Christopher Vials (London: Verso, 2020), 269.

20. Compare Black Panther Party, "Call for a United Front against Fascism," 269 and Dimitrov, *The Fascist Offensive and Unity of the Working Class*, 5.

21. Dimitrov, *The Fascist Offensive*, 3.

22. Dimitrov, *The Fascist Offensive*, 5–6.

23. Dimitrov, *The Fascist Offensive*, 6.

24. Dimitrov, *The Fascist Offensive*, 6.

25. Robert Paxton, *The Anatomy of Fascism* (New York: Vintage, 2005), 94.

26. Dimitrov, *The Fascist Offensive*, 6.

27. Noel Ignatiev (writing as Noel Ignatin), "Fascism: Some Common Misconceptions," *Urgent Tasks* 4 (Summer 1978): 25.

28. The Black Panther Party, "Call for a United Front against Fascism," 268.

29. Kathleen Cleaver, "Racism, Fascism, and Political Murder" [September 14, 1968], in Mullen and Vials, *The U.S. Antifascism Reader*, 264, 266.

30. Vials, *Haunted by Hitler*, 176.

31. Mumia Abu-Jamal, *We Want Freedom: A Life in the Black Panther Party* (Cambridge, Mass: South End Press, 2004), 208–9.

32. Abu-Jamal, *We Want Freedom*, 208.

33. Abu-Jamal, *We Want Freedom*, 210.

34. Cleaver, "Racism, Fascism, and Political Murder," 266.

35. Marx, "The Civil War in France," in *The First International and After: Political Writings*, vol. 3, ed. David Fernbach (London: Penguin, 1974), 207.

36. Robin D.G. Kelley, *Hammer and Hoe: Alabama Communists during the Great Depression*, 25th anniversary edition (Chapel Hill: UNC Press, 2015), xx.

37. For example, Vials asserts—despite writing after the heyday of Anti-Racist Action—that "the queer antifascisms of the 1980s and early 1990s [embodied in ACT UP and other groups] marked the last point in American history in which this discourse [antifascism] was used in a sustained, concentrated manner by a left-oriented social movement." His claim only makes sense if we understand his analysis to focus exclusively on groups which attempted to exercise parliamentary pressure. See *Haunted by Hitler*, 232.

38. See John Riddell, ed., *Toward the United Front: Proceedings of the Fourth Congress of the Communist International, 1922* (Chicago: Haymarket Books, 2012), 1154.

39. Dimitrov, *The Fascist Offensive*, 7.

40. Dimitrov, *The Fascist Offensive*, 19.

41. Dimitrov, *The Fascist Offensive*, 7.

42. See Torkil Lauesen, *The Global Perspective: Reflections on Imperialism and Resistance* (Montreal: Kersplebedeb, 2018), 130–42.

43. Dimitrov, *The Fascist Offensive*, 33. Kelley documents the ramifications of this shift for communist organizing in Alabama in *Hammer and Hoe*.

44. Dimitrov, *The Fascist Offensive*, 66.

45. Dimitrov, *The Fascist Offensive*, 19.

46. See Griffin, *The Nature of Fascism*, 37: "Ultra-nationalism" means forms of nationalism "which 'go beyond,' and hence reject, anything compatible with liberal institutions or with the tradition of Enlightenment humanism which underpins them."

47. Griffin, *The Nature of Fascism*, 37.

48. Dimitrov, *The Fascist Offensive*, on sexism: 55–56; on the policy of sterilization: 10.

49. Dimitrov, *The Fascist Offensive*, 32.

50. Sakai, "The Shock of Recognition," 130. We should be careful not to read this evocation of "need" as a repetition of the top-down view of fascism held by the orthodox line.

51. Du Bois threw his support behind World War I in 1919. Alberto Toscano undertakes a comparative reading of Du Bois and Lenin, while explaining Du Bois's about face as the result of a "painful entanglement of two partially-overlapping colour lines: the one cutting through the U.S. working class, the other dividing white and non-white labour globally." See Toscano, "'America's Belgium': W.E.B. Du Bois on Race, Class, and the Origins of World War I," in Alexander Anievas, ed., *Cataclysm 1914: The First World War and the Making of Modern Politics* (Chicago: Haymarket Books, 2016), 238–39.

52. V. I. Lenin, "Imperialism and the Split in Socialism," in *Collected Works* [hereafter CW] 23 (Moscow: Progress Publishers, 1960–1970): 114–15. The essays I cite from Lenin are collected in the more accessible volume originally compiled by the Communist Working Circle in 1972 and reprinted with an introduction by Torkil Lauesen, *V.I. Lenin: On Imperialism and Opportunism* (Montreal: Kersplebedeb, 2019).

53. V. I. Lenin, "The Collapse of the Second International" (1915), CW 21, 244, my emphasis.

54. Lenin, "Imperialism and the Split in Socialism," CW 23, 115–16.

55. W.E.B. Du Bois, "The African Roots of War" (1915), reprinted in *Monthly Review* 24, no. 11 (1973): 34.

56. Lenin, "Second Congress," CW 31, 230.

57. Lenin, "Second Congress," CW 31, 230.

58. Lauesen, *The Global Perspective*, 132.

59. Du Bois, *Black Reconstruction in America* (Oxford: Oxford University Press, 2007), 573–74.

60. Du Bois, "Marxism and the Negro Problem," in *Writings in Periodicals Edited by W.E.B. Du Bois: Selections from The Crisis*, vol. 2: 1926–1934 (Millwood, NY: Kraus-Thomson, 1983), 698.

61. Kevin Bruyneel, *Settler Memory: The Disavowal of Indigeneity and the Politics of Race in the United States* (Chapel Hill: UNC Press, 2021), 62.

62. Boggs, however, saw American fascism as an exception to the typical functioning of fascist movements (namely, the former is grassroots while the latter is top down): "Fascism in the United States is therefore unique in that it is grass roots rather than from the top down. Today the Minute Men, America Firsters, White Citizens' Councils, and the scores

of other white organizations organized to defend the United States from the demands of blacks for justice are made up of workers, skilled and unskilled, who work every day alongside blacks in the shop and then night after night organize in the suburbs against these same blacks." See *Racism and the Class Struggle: Further Pages from a Black Worker's Notebook* (New York: Monthly Review Press, 1970), 96.

II. Militancy and Critique

4. Fighting Fascism with Feminism: A Review of Tammy Kovich's *Anti-Fascism Against Machismo*

Combatting the rise of far-right and fascist social mobilization is an urgent task for militant antifascists. Whereas liberal antifascists place a naive and unfounded faith in civil society and law enforcement to apply normative and legal force to permanently marginalize far-right movements, militant antifascists fight these movements through direct action and a diversity of tactics; for the latter, it is a question of meeting organizing with organizing. Militant antifascists engage in information campaigns to place pressure on liberal institutions to deny a platform to fascists; they dox anonymous or pseudonymous far-right organizers to out them to the communities where they live and work; and when the far right mobilizes in the streets, to harass and

This text originally appeared on the Social Justice Centre blog, January 5, 2020. The original review discussed the pamphlet written under the pseudonym Petronella Lee, published by The Tower InPrint, also available online at https://north-shore.info/2019/10/03/anti-fascism-beyond-machismo/. For ease of reference, all page numbers cited in this chapter are to the edition published by Kersplebedeb in 2023: Tammy Kovich et al., *Anti-Fascism against Machismo* (Montreal: Kersplebedeb, 2023). Kovich's text is also included as a chapter in Xtn Alexander and Matthew N. Lyons, eds., *Three Way Fight: Revolutionary Politics and Antifascism* (Montreal/Oakland: Kersplebedeb/PM Press, 2024), 71–105.

intimidate our communities, militant antifascists meet them with a diversity of tactics.

Given that over the past four years far-right street-level mobilizations have organized around publicly explicit white nationalism, racism, and xenophobia, antifascists have often focused on antiracist organizing—in militant forms of street mobilization and forms of community outreach, self-defense, and coalition-building. But the far right isn't only white supremacist and racist. In general, in the context of the United States and Canada, we could functionally define the far right and fascism as forms of populist social mobilization that demand the re-entrenchment of the economic and social hierarchies that have enabled and furthered the project of white settler-colonialism. These hierarchies include class stratification, heteropatriarchy, ableism, and white supremacist racisms (plural here, given how differing types of racism—anti-Blackness, anti-Indigeneity, antisemitism, Islamophobia—play different roles in far-right ideology).

While there are debates concerning the exact class composition of far-right movements, it is generally acknowledged that the bourgeoisie and fascist movements typically ally against socialist or communist social forces. And while it is generally acknowledged that racism plays a formative role in the ultra-nationalist populism of the far right, some aspects of racism remain undertheorized. (For example, the relationship between American and Canadian far-right notions of a white homeland and the apparatuses of the broader settler-colonial project— on this point, Rowland "Enāēmaehkiw" Keshena Robinson's "Fascism and Anti-Fascism: A Decolonial Perspective" remains indispensable.)[1]

Anti-Fascism Against Machismo, then, is a timely and important contribution toward understanding, to paraphrase the subtitle, gender and politics in the struggle against fascism. The essay, first published by Tammy Kovich under the pseudonym Petronella Lee, is (in the original pamphlet) a brief but engaging forty-two pages, divided into three parts. In Part One, Kovich

examines the gender politics of fascism and the ways that liberal feminism has failed to interrogate the white supremacist
underpinnings of its call for state protections of (white) women
and (some parts of) LGBTQ+ communities. In Part Two, she
sketches a short, episodic history of women's antifascist activity, focusing on movements in Ethiopia (during Italian colonization), the Spanish Civil War, and partisan resistance against
Nazi occupation in Yugoslavia. In Part Three, Kovich draws on
these histories to outline seven insights for an explicitly feminist
antifascism. She concludes by calling for a militant antifascism
critical of machismo.

In *Insurgent Supremacists*: *The U.S. Far Right's Challenge to
State and Empire* (2018), Matthew N. Lyons categorizes gender
and sexuality as "neglected themes" in the analysis and criticism
of the far right, though Kovich's meticulous citation apparatus
shows how extensively its sexism, misogyny, and transphobia
has been documented by researchers and journalists. In other
words, the far right's adherence to masculinist gender hierarchies has been documented, but it is not always clear how these
groups coalesce, or splinter, around the role of women within the
movement. Lyons, for his part, identifies four ideological themes
present in the far right: "patriarchal traditionalism," which promotes rigid gender roles typically based on a patriarchal family structure; "demographic nationalism," which maintains that
women's main duty is to have children for the nation or race;
"male bonding through warfare," which emphasizes warfare,
combat, and martial values as a bonding mechanism between
men (and which implicitly or explicitly celebrates homoeroti-
cism and male homosexuality); and "quasi-feminism," which
advocates specific rights for women (typically) of the privileged
nation or race but maintains nonetheless that male dominance
is natural and immutable.[2] After drawing these distinctions, he
catalogues how these themes are manifested, sometimes coexist-
ing in tenuous and contradictory ways, in various movements in
the United States. There's a risk, though, despite the attention
to empirical detail, that the reader comes away from *Insurgent*

Supremacists without a clear account of how these far-right positions on gender hierarchy cohere and converge and where they opportunistically seek to normalize their views.

On this point, Kovich's analysis is incisive. Despite their disagreements, far-right movements share three common assumptions: first, that gender is a biologically determined fact; second, that gender is binary and each gender carries "innate traits and predetermined characteristics" that "inescapably dictat[e] one's place in the world"; and third, that there is a gender hierarchy where men are fundamentally superior to women. In sum: "gender is determined by nature, gender differences are immutable, and a clear gender hierarchy where men dominate and rule exists (and is desirable)" (39). Furthermore, while there are competing ideological trends, Kovich contends that these split, practically speaking, into two groups around the role that women ought to play within far-right movements: what she calls *patriarchal fascism* and *misogynistic fascism*. Both tendencies consider women to be inferior to men, but the former assigns positive but restricted roles to women's activities. By contrast, "many contemporary groups influenced by the Alt Right promote an intensely misogynistic ideology that straight-up hates women" (42). According to misogynistic fascism, women have no positive role to play within far-right movements.

These categories are important for identifying trajectories of convergence and divergence within the far right. While examples of misogyny abound in the Alt Right and associated groups, Kovich documents how it underpins the far more extreme Daily Stormer website (which bans women from contributing to the site) and the accelerationist Atomwaffen Division, whose members promote rape as a terrorist tool (43). We might consider, then, that misogynistic fascism functions as a path of violent radicalization within the movement; at the same time, it appears to be one ideological and organizational fault-line between older and newer white supremacist movements—Kovich notes, for example, that The Daily Stormer's position has brought it into conflict with women associated with Stormfront.

It is also important to note, despite their differences, how the common assumptions about gender shared by the far right translate into

> agreement on opposing the notion of gender as non-binary, and thus, agreement on opposing (and frequently enacting violence against) genderqueer and trans people. In general, the far-right shares revulsion for trans people, and a particular hostility for trans-women who "are seen as men who reject their natural roles and privileges and 'voluntarily' become the hated other." (39)

I believe there is a missed opportunity here, for Kovich could have returned to this point in her later discussion of how liberal feminist calls for safety re-entrench or expand the apparatuses of the "racialized penal state" (a discussion found in the section "White Supremacy, Complicity, and the Legacy of Saviour Politics"). There, Kovich contends that liberal calls for safety and security for women typically draw on or leave unexamined racist tropes (the racialized Other who poses a threat to white women) and sanction expanded police powers. She notes how racist and xenophobic groups have disingenuously feigned support for feminist groups and LGBTQ+ groups as a way of normalizing their far-right views. But Kovich does not address how the far right could pursue a path for recruitment and normalization through trans-exclusionary reactionary feminism (*sic*). Both movements share essentializing and binaristic assumptions about gender, and both opportunistically exploit the safety/security discourse to present non-binary and transgender women as threats to (white) ciswomen and children (and in terms obviously indebted to homophobic discourses from the 1990s). I would suggest that where explicit racism fails to provide a path to normalization, we can expect far-right movements to regroup — as opportunistic proponents for so-called free speech — around public presentations of transmisogyny.[3]

Kovich concludes by outlining a path toward a militant feminist antifascism between, on the one hand, a liberal feminism, reliant on the state for security and beholden to "a dead end of permitted marches, electoral campaigns, and 'pussy hat'" political symbolism, and, on the other, currents of antifascist organizing which tend toward "bravado and dogmatic combativity" (74). Militant antifascism is, of course, distinguished from liberal antifascism by a willingness to use direct action and a diversity of tactics to combat far-right mobilizations. Kovich observes, however, that antifascist groups are continually at risk of replacing a commitment to respecting a diversity of tactics with a "political position that prioritizes confrontation while it more or less ignores (or at least downplays) other aspects of struggle" (74). At the same time, this antifascist machismo "reproduces some of the worst characteristics of hegemonic masculinity with a self-righteous zeal, and considers discussion of things like sexism to be needlessly divisive and a distraction from the 'important things'" (74).

Here, Kovich identifies two major *organizational* problems which are often treated as *ideological* problems. The first problem involves treating a diversity of tactics as a hierarchy of tactics, in which physical combat takes priority over other forms of activity; this is compounded when groups default to placing men in prominent organizational and leadership roles based on their willingness to physically confront fascists. Physical confrontation is typically a small part of antifascist work and is most effective when integrated within a political strategy that aims to undermine and fragment far-right organizing. Therefore, as Kovich notes, antifascist work also requires public education, labor and community organizing and outreach, information gathering, building movement infrastructure, and creating a broader antifascist political culture (68). Done effectively, each of these forms of organizing places a substantial social cost on participation in far-right movements.

The second problem occurs when critiques of sexism and machismo are relegated to secondary, largely ideological concerns. By contrast, Kovich maintains that "gender liberation [is] a non-negotiable component of anti-fascism. This means centering gender considerations, taking trans politics and queer struggle seriously, and not treating these things as peripheral concerns" (70). Kovich makes the case that sexism is a fundamentally organizational concern, which can affect internal decision-making dynamics and community outreach. She notes that, for example, in building an antifascist political culture, "we cannot focus almost exclusively on physical activities and/or traditional male-dominated spaces"; instead, we must also cultivate reading groups, social clubs, collective kitchens, daycare centers, and workplace organizations (69). These activities and organizations must be attentive to ability and age; as Kovich writes, "a vibrant movement would have a place for [a] two-year-old child up to their eighty-two-year-old grandparent" (75).

Furthermore, we must be cognizant of gender stereotyping in internal organizing initiatives. In a movement committed to a diversity of tactics, one must criticize machismo but also stereotypical assumptions that identify violence with masculinity: "against the tendency to associate women with passivity and non-violence, it is crucial to recognize that combative politics is not exclusively the domain of men" (69). Kovich's point is especially salient for organizations involved in community self-defense initiatives. Self-defense involves both practical training and political education. From the latter angle, antifascists must articulate a critical perspective that attacks the white, masculine, settler-colonial imaginary which underlies the default North American concept of an individual's right to self-defense.[4] (And here an education in the history of Black armed community self-defense during the Civil Rights Era is instructive.)[5] This political education must be met in practice by self-defense awareness training for street mobilizations that involve collective defense against both fascists and police, but also for the community at large, where skills in conflict de-escalation and resolution are more useful and necessary than physical violence. Antifascists who participate in these types of self-defense initiatives ought to be trained in a diversity of tactics while being vigilant against lapsing into divisions of labor anchored in gender stereotypes.

It is readily recognized within all revolutionary currents of militant antifascism that fascism cannot be defeated until the conditions that make it possible are overthrown. For this reason, antifascists are anti-capitalist and antiracist. There is a growing awareness that in North America there is no meaningful way that fascism will be defeated without decolonization. Kovich demonstrates not only that gender oppression is one of the fundamental pillars of fascism but also that gender liberation must be a non-negotiable component of antifascism.

NOTES

1. See Rowland "Enāēmaehkiw" Keshena Robinson, "Fascism and Anti-Fascism: A Decolonial Perspective," *Maehkōn Ahpēhtesewen*, February 11, 2017 [Edited 2019.] This essay is also included in Xtn Alexander and Matthew N. Lyons, eds., *Three Way Fight: Revolutionary Politics and Antifascism* (Montreal/Oakland: Kersplebedeb/PM Press, 2024), 53–70.

2. Lyons, *Insurgent Supremacists*, 94–95.

3. Indeed, we might also expect that "free speech" would constitute a point of convergence that carries "plausible deniability" for TERFs who build coalitions with, but for optics do not publicly or explicitly endorse, far-right groups.

4. This critique is central to the contributions collected in scott crow, ed., *Setting Sights: Histories and Reflections on Community and Armed Self-Defense* (Oakland: PM Press, 2018).

5. For a good, recent introduction to this history, see Charles E. Cobb, Jr., *This Nonviolent Stuff'll Get You Killed: How Guns Made the Civil Rights Movement Possible* (Durham: Duke University Press, 2016).

5. The Limits of Liberal Antifascism: A Review of Jason Stanley's *How Fascism Works*

Jason Stanley's *How Fascism Works: The Politics of Us and Them* is a succinct book of philosophy written for a popular audience.[1] It might be the best-known contemporary book on fascism by a philosopher, if not the best-known contemporary liberal antifascist critique of fascism. Stanley focuses on how "fascist tactics [are used] as a mechanism to achieve power" (xiv). He identifies a number of (often overlapping) discursive tactics common to fascist movements, all of which function to distinguish a community ("us") against outsiders ("them") based on supposed ethnic, religious, or racial differences. Each chapter is dedicated to one tactic: the trope of the mythic past, the use of propaganda, anti-intellectualism, the erosion of common standards of reasoned debate, anti-egalitarianism, the cultivation of victimhood, law and order rhetoric, the sexual anxieties of heteropatriarchy, anti-cosmopolitanism, and fascist attitudes toward work (in short, their false theory of producerism and their opposition to unions). Many of these themes will be familiar to scholars and activists fighting fascism, and the point-by-point organization of the argument is similar to Umberto Eco's "Ur-Fascism."[2] Nonetheless, *How Fascism Works* fails to integrate its compendium of instances of fascist tactics and wide erudition

---

Originally published by *Marx and Philosophy Review of Books*, May 13, 2020.

into a compelling and complete account of how fascism works and, *crucially*, how to fight it.

There are numerous threads within his argument that pose philosophical problems that Stanley fails to resolve. Instead, they are truncated by an assumption that is challenged by his own subsequent references and citations. He writes: "I have written this book in the hope of providing citizens with the critical tools to recognize the difference between legitimate tactics in liberal democratic politics on the one hand, and invidious tactics in fascist politics on the other" (xvi). But we should reject the assumption that there is a clear demarcation between legitimate liberal norms and illegitimate fascist tactics — especially in a settler-colonial society built on the pillars of Black slavery and Indigenous genocide and dispossession. Given the long coexistence of liberalism and settler-colonialism, a better application of liberal norms is not enough to extirpate the threat of fascism. Instead, we need to extirpate the conditions that make fascism in countries such as the United States or Canada possible: settler colonialism and capitalism themselves.

Though Stanley asserts a distinction between liberal norms and fascist politics, he himself builds a case that upends the assumption that there is a clear line demarcating liberalism and, given that *fascism* is a misleading term in this context, the systemic white supremacy that animates and perpetuates settler-colonialism. Upending this assumption is crucial, because there is a not-insignificant portion of his readership who might be given to the belief that the threat of fascism is extinguished if Donald Trump is defeated in the next presidential election.

Stanley's analytic method lapses into anachronism. By *analytic*, it can be understood that the author begins with a definition of fascism and then identifies which tropes, rhetoric, or discourses are fascist on the basis of this definition. He defines fascism as "ultranationalism of some variety (ethnic, religious, cultural), with the nation represented in the person of an authoritarian leader who speaks on its behalf," and thus typically those statements that fulfil some condition(s) of this definition are henceforth considered to be fascist (xvi). Even if we grant that this definition correctly identifies fascism as an ideology, it omits any discussion of that feature which distinguishes it from something like a "merely" ultranationalist dictatorship: a relatively autonomous and insurgent (potentially) mass base. We will return to this problem, but for the moment suffice it to say that once fascist rhetoric is untethered from its historical conditions, it becomes more difficult to disambiguate it from other forms of racism, heteropatriarchy, and xenophobia. This problem, which is manifest in Stanley's anachronism, undermines our ability to formulate how to fight fascism and systemic forms of oppression, because organizing to combat far-right social movements and organizing to fight systemic forms of oppression call for different strategies.

Stanley makes three notable anachronistic moves in his discussion of fascism, each of which refers to an instance of nineteenth-century American racism. The first occurs in Chapter 2, in the midst of a discussion of fascist propaganda. He notes that in the antebellum period, Americans commonly celebrated the United States as a beacon of liberty, despite the ongoing dispossession of Indigenous peoples and Black slavery, because they shared the belief that these nonwhite peoples "were not suitable recipients of the goods of liberty" (30). He then immediately remarks that "this is classic fascist ideology with a hierarchy of value of worth between races" (30). Next, in Chapter 4, when discussing how fascist ideology asserts social hierarchies as the product of natural law, he analyzes the speech, now known as the "Cornerstone Speech," that Alexander H. Stephens (the vice president of the Confederacy) delivered in 1861. Finally, in Chapter 6, while outlining how fascism cultivates the perception of victimhood among "dominant groups at the prospect of sharing citizenship and power with minorities," his first illustration of this phenomenon references Andrew Johnson's justification for vetoing the Civil Rights Act of 1866 (95). Stanley observes: "As W.E.B. Du Bois notes, Johnson perceived minimal safeguards at the start of a path toward future black equality as 'discrimination against the white race'" (93).

The crux of the present intervention rests on how we interpret these anachronistic references to nineteenth-century American racism as fascism. They are anachronistic because, while numerous scholars categorize the first Ku Klux Klan (founded in 1865) as proto-fascist, Stanley draws the historical timeline backwards, past Johnson, past the Confederate Stephens, back to antebellum American ideology writ large — which is not a historical periodization shared within the scholarly consensus about fascism. It might be defensible (though, I believe, still wrong) if he provided argumentation in favor of this reclassification, but he does not. Indeed, he doesn't acknowledge the anachronism. If we were more analytically-inclined (in the sense of the philosophical school), we might accept that Johnson or Stephens used fascist tactics but then debate how many instances of fascist tactics are sufficient for a fascist movement, but from our perspective such a debate makes two fatal mistakes. First, it conflates the conditions that make fascism possible in North America with fascism itself; i.e., it conflates settler-colonialism and anti-Black racism with fascism, when the former are some of the conditions that make the latter possible. Second, such a debate assumes that fascist ideological tactics are *sufficient* for the emergence of fascism, which occludes an analysis of fascism as an insurgent (potentially) mass social movement.

We might suggest an alternative, militant approach derived in part from the work of W.E.B. Du Bois, which is also a frequent point of reference in Stanley's book. Although Stanley cites both *Darkwater* (1920) and *Black Reconstruction* (1935), he does not engage with the earlier book's discussion of "the souls of white folk" and summarizes only in passing the description of the "public and psychological wage" of whiteness in *Black Reconstruction* (21–23). In *Darkwater*, Du Bois proposes that whiteness is a social category that signals both a right to dominion, sovereignty, or ownership (consider, for example, what grounds settler colonialism has for dispossessing Indigenous

land *other* than assertions of white supremacy) and an entitlement to access to political and cultural power (access to presti-
gious forms of work or education). Furthermore, Du Bois argues
that whiteness as we know it is the result of a late nineteenth-
century and early twentieth-century political compromise between the bourgeoisie and the white working-class *against* the
"darker peoples" around the globe — and, in a nutshell, this interpellation of "personal whiteness" animates far-right and fascist
movements.

There is a burgeoning literature within Indigenous Studies
and Critical Race Theory that begins from a critique of whiteness along the lines suggested by Du Bois, which demonstrates
how whiteness as possession and entitlement functions in the
ongoing dispossession of Indigenous peoples and anti-Black
racism. In the American context, Cheryl Harris observes that
"after legalized segregation was overturned, whiteness as property evolved into a more modern form through the law's ratification of the settled expectations of relative white privilege
as a *legitimate and natural baseline.*"[3] In addition, some prison
abolitionists have argued that the Prison Industrial Complex
perpetuates the caste system of American segregation in a new
form of Jim Crow.

A truly emancipatory, militant antifascism must reckon with
the conclusions of these fields and movements in both our organizing and our critique of fascism. Though Stanley touches on
these themes, he nonetheless truncates his analysis of fascism,
severing it from its settler-colonial roots. As a result, on the
one hand, he conflates some institutional features of the North
American settler-colonial project with fascism, while on the
other, he inflates the antifascist credentials of contemporary liberal norms. By contrast, I contend that settler-state hegemony is
constituted through a compromise between liberalism (or bourgeois democracy) and the forces of white supremacy.

In general, the present system of institutionalized white supremacy, capital accumulation, racism, and heteropatriarchy
poses a greater danger to our communities than the insurgent

forces of fascist movements. But I also maintain that fascism emerges as a dangerous social force, with some degree of relative autonomy within broader settler-colonial hegemony, when white settlers perceive that their interests are no longer advanced by bourgeois institutions. I propose, therefore, the following thesis on the relationship between the far right and settler colonialism: *Far-right movements are system-loyal when they perceive that the entitlements of white supremacy can be advanced within bourgeois or democratic institutions, and they become insurgent when they perceive that these entitlements cannot.* But whether they are system-loyal or insurgent, far-right and fascist movements demand the intensification and re-entrenchment of the settler-colonial project itself. There is no meaningful sense in which fascism can be defeated without overthrowing the conditions that make it possible—in North America, these include capital accumulation and settler colonialism. Given their long historical imbrication in settler colonialism, merely appealing for a return to liberal norms and ideals won't make that happen.

NOTES

1. Jason Stanley, *How Fascism Works: The Politics of Us and Them* (New York: Random House, 2018).

2. Umberto Eco, "Ur-Fascism," *The New York Review of Books,* June 22, 1995.

3. Cheryl Harris, "Whiteness as Property," *Harvard Law Review* 106, no. 8 (1993): 1714.

6. On Alberto Toscano's Critique of "Racial Fascism"

Alberto Toscano's "The Long Shadow of Racial Fascism," can be situated within a broader reconsideration of fascism in light of colonialism, settler colonialism, and the Prison Industrial Complex (hereafter PIC). [1] His work is part of an antifascist current which is rightly critical of the mainstream discussion among liberal intellectuals, whose analyses of the far right and the Trump administration tend to rely on analogies between the present conjuncture and German and Italian fascism, eliciting — at least on social media — poor comparisons between current events and prospective Reichstag fires or the collapse of the Weimar Republic. While Toscano highlights the importance of including the Black Radical Tradition's critique of the PIC in antifascist thought, his account does not situate his concepts of "racial fascism" or "late fascism" (analogically modeled on the concepts of "racial capitalism" and "late capitalism") within a three way fight framework.

The mainstream liberal view often presents the recent rise of the far right and so-called "Trumpism" as a marked departure from prior American politics. Toscano, drawing on the Black Radical Tradition, argues that recent events are deeply rooted in colonialism, settler colonialism, and anti-Black racism. He shows that a number of Black intellectuals in the 1930s, such as

Originally published on the *Three Way Fight* website, December 30, 2020.

George Padmore and Langston Hughes, had demonstrated the family resemblance—though, importantly, not outright identity—between settler colonialism and European fascism.

We will focus here on Toscano's reading of W.E.B. Du Bois's *Black Reconstruction*, a "monumental reckoning with the history of U.S. racial capitalism." His interpretation of Du Bois uncritically accepts an understanding of fascism that blocks an appreciation of the three way fight. Toscano argues that the overthrow of Reconstruction enacted a "racial fascism" that long predated Hitlerism in its use of racial terror, conscription of poor whites, and manipulation by "the most reactionary, most chauvinistic, and most imperialist sector of finance capital" (to quote the famous definition of fascism by Georgi Dimitrov).

Toscano's interpretation of *Black Reconstruction* results in a reductive view of Du Bois's concept of the public and psychological wages of whiteness. Though *Black Reconstruction* and Dimitrov's speeches on fascism both date from 1935, they present starkly different directions in antiracist and antifascist praxis. Dimitrov posited a narrow view of fascism as the most reactionary faction of capital in order to legitimate a Popular Front policy, which allowed communists to organize with social democrats and factions of the bourgeoisie that opposed their most reactionary peers.

In the United States, the Popular Front also led to a shift in the Communist Party USA's position on Black liberation, from self-determination to civil rights. And even though Dimitrov's speeches called for the mass antifascist party in the U.S. to fight for the equal status of Black Americans, their interests were, as Robin D.G. Kelley observes in his study of communist organizing in interwar Alabama, effectively sidelined in Communist Party work during the Popular Front period.[2] While the Black Panther Party later adopted the popular front line under its leadership as a Black vanguard party (hence, I believe, Toscano's invocation of it), the claim that fascism is rooted in the most reactionary faction of capitalism came to be paired, via George Jackson, with focoist underground armed resistance severed from mass organizing. We should keep these historical pitfalls in mind when developing our own antifascist praxis.

For Du Bois, the wages of whiteness functioned to establish a broad recomposition of settler-state hegemony across class lines, including the white bourgeoisie, petty bourgeoisie, and working class. (I will explain settler-state hegemony below.) But the wages of whiteness did more than merely align racial interests against class interests. Here, we step from *Black Reconstruction* to Kwando Mbiassi Kinshasa's *Black Resistance to the Ku Klux Klan in the Wake of Civil War* (2006). As is well-known, white racists formed clandestine system-oppositional groups (such as the first Ku Klux Klan), which carried out terror in the Reconstruction South. Kinshasa shows how, in response, Black Southerners engaged in community self-defense. On this basis, we may also conclude that the recomposition of settler-colonial hegemony around the wages of whiteness also pulled system-oppositional white racists within a system-loyal paradigm while effectively disarming Black opposition to racism and Jim Crow.

For Du Bois, the hegemony that coalesces around the wages of whiteness marked the defeat of what he called "abolition democracy" by Northern industrialists and Southern whites. In terms of the three way fight, his account differentiates between abolition democracy, system-loyal Northerners, and system-oppositional Southerners. What Toscano calls "racial fascism" would be part of a broad hegemony and not merely the most reactionary faction of capital. But Toscano doesn't necessarily evoke Dimitrov to the letter. More accurately, Toscano adapts Dimitrov's line in order to treat racial fascism as a form of "extreme" capitalism (or "late fascism," which is as problematic a term as the "post-fascism" used by others)—that is as an extreme form of the capitalist system rather than as a reactionary or extreme *faction* of the bourgeoisie.

Given that contemporary forms of the system-oppositional far right emerged conditioned by, and in response to, the ascendency of neoliberalism and the PIC, Toscano is correct to return to criticisms of the PIC developed by George Jackson and Angela Y. Davis (among others). More specifically, modern forms of the far right and fascism are a reaction to liberation struggles, "preventive counterreform" even. However, it becomes especially important to untangle counterrevolutionary forces without conflating them. Thus, it would be necessary to disentangle state power—embodied here in the development of the PIC within generally liberal legal parameters—and its relationship to white supremacy: both how neoliberal hegemony coalesces around "law and order" and how, despite this recomposition of whiteness and hegemony, far-right groups on the ground shift toward system-oppositional currents in the late 1970s and early 1980s. The latter details escape the horizon of Toscano's account.

Instead, Toscano returns to his initial challenge to liberal antifascists. On the basis of Jackson and Davis, he contends that the growth of the PIC is not a departure from liberal governance but part and parcel of its modern form. But his schematic assertions remain problematic. For example, he argues:

> This [a view that accepts George Jackson's and Angela Davis's concept of fascism] both echoes and departs from the Black radical theories of fascism, such as Padmore's or Césaire's, which emerged from the experience of the colonized. The new, U.S. fascism that Jackson and Davis strive to delineate is not an unwanted return from the "other scene" of colonial violence, but originates from liberal democracy itself.

On the one hand, over the last few years there has been a well-warranted revival of interest in Aimé Césaire's *Discourse on Colonialism*, but his observation that fascism was imperialist violence turned back upon Europe does not accurately describe how fascism is conditioned by a settler-colonial society. On the other hand, Toscano's account also incorrectly posits a false distinction between the "other scene" of colonial violence and liberal democracy in order to assert the continuity between liberal democracy and fascism. The distinction is false because settler colonialism—the dispossession and oppression of Indigenous peoples—is not beyond the borders of and historically prior to liberal democracy but occurs within it and is ongoing.

Thus, I contend that a three way fight perspective must examine how settler-state hegemony coalesces between liberalism and white supremacy, or between the interests of capital and white settlerism, so that militant antifascism can successfully fight both. In other words, an analysis of the far right and fascism in North America must maintain an analytic distinction between liberalism and white supremacy even though there is a constantly moving dialectical relationship between them. They converge through some common interests and diverge on others.

We have seen how, according to Du Bois, these interests converged through the wages of whiteness (although his account must be modified to incorporate how the white settlement of the western frontier played a part in the formation of post-Reconstruction hegemony). They have diverged more recently, for example, when liberal factions of settler-state hegemony have extended formal protections for minorities demanded by civil rights movements. In response, far-right groups have turned toward system-oppositional forms of organization.

In general, I assert that far-right movements are system-loyal when they perceive that the entitlements of white supremacy can be advanced within bourgeois or democratic institutions, and they become insurgent when they perceive that these entitlements cannot. On this basis, we cannot collapse the reactionary dimension of the PIC into the reaction of system-oppositional far-right movements. I would suggest that the far-right street movements defending the thin blue line remain in need of interpretation—what actual material benefits accrue to them for rallying to the side of the police? What symbolic or ideological needs are met here? Why do some far-right groups ally with state power and others reject it?

We will conclude by revisiting Toscano's claim that fascism is a form of "preventive counterreform." It is a longstanding view, at least since Clara Zetkin's essay "The Struggle against Fascism,"[3] that fascism emerges on the basis of the failure of the revolutionary left. Given that the left lacks the strength it had many decades ago, it is more accurate to describe the recent far-right reaction as preventive counterreform, attempting to block the formation of a mass militant antifascist, antiracist, and anticapitalist movement from growing out of the anti-police uprising during 2020. And here Toscano's account fails us; it ends without outlining any conclusions for antifascist practice. In my view, this failure occurs because he has identified fascism as a political or state form of "extreme" capitalism, which collapses antifascism into the struggle against this system. By contrast, militant antifascism has to organize against both far-right street movements and capitalism.

Indeed, the present crisis also runs deeper than terminological choices like "preventive counterreform" imply. There were, this summer and fall (2020), widespread antifascist and antiracist struggles against both policing and insurgent right-wing groups. The police and the far right sometimes took up tactical alliances (even if this was merely law enforcement looking the other way when far-right groups went on the attack), and, in other cases, policing turned against these groups (we can see this in the federal law enforcement crackdown against the boogaloo bois and others).

As I have argued in Chapter 2, "Between System-Loyal Vigilantism and System-Oppositional Violence," during the fall of 2020 it was uncertain whether far-right groups would align as system-loyal or system-oppositional after the U.S. presidential election. It was possible that the election would result in a reorganization of settler-state hegemony with a more prominent public and perhaps institutional role for far-right organizing. Although I thought it unlikely, I did not want to minimize the danger of this possibility. The other possibility, that the far right would be pushed organizationally back toward system-opposition, appears to have been the result of Trump's 2020 defeat—though, of course, along the way the Republican Party has witnessed the further growth of far-right tendencies.

Toscano helps highlight the counterrevolutionary threat of the still-present mechanisms of the PIC and other state apparatuses, but the far right as a system-oppositional movement remains beyond his analytic horizon. While liberal antifascists, on his account, cannot naively congratulate themselves for defeating fascism by electing Biden, Toscano's own position remains similarly detached from a practical relationship to ongoing militant antifascist movements.

NOTES

1. Alberto Toscano, "The Long Shadow of Racial Fascism," *Boston Review*, October 28, 2020.

2. Surveying Communist Party USA organizing in Alabama, Robin D.G. Kelley argues that the Party "practically ceased to function as an independent, autonomous organization ... the failure of the CIO's Operation Dixie, anticommunism within the AFL-CIO, not to mention the anticommunism of the NAACP, weakened or destroyed the Communist-led unions, leaving an indelible mark on the next wave of civil rights activists and possibly arresting what may have been a broader economic and social justice agenda." Kelley, *Hammer and Hoe*, xx.

3. See Clara Zetkin, *Fighting Fascism: How to Struggle and How to Win*, ed. Mike Taber and John Riddell (Chicago: Haymarket Books, 2017).

7. A Review of K. Murali (Ajith), *Critiquing Brahmanism: A Collection of Essays*

The theory and practice of the three way fight was developed by militant antifascists to differentiate between the threats posed to leftist movements by relatively autonomous insurgent far-right and fascist movements and forms of oppression exercised through systems of capital accumulation, bourgeois rule, and the attendant state repressive apparatus. This approach rejects the still prevalent view among the left that typically treats far-right movements as the puppets of the most extreme factions of capitalism. Some adherents of the three way fight consider how "fascism has the potential to become a mass movement with a substantial and genuine element of revolutionary anti-capitalism."[1] Others acknowledge the threat of this mass potential but contend that far-right movements are more specifically opposed to liberal forms of political and cultural power (such as recent aspirations toward inclusiveness or protections for minority rights) rather than being revolutionary or anticapitalist. Despite these theoretical debates, adherents of the three way fight generally agree on the practical terms of North American militant antifascism: it is a defensive form of organizing oriented against both far-right street movements and state power in its ideological and repressive forms—liberal "repressive tolerance" and police forces.

Originally published by the *Marx and Philosophy Review of Books*, Dec. 9, 2020.

In what follows, I will draw parallels between Ajith's critique of Brahmanism and the perspective of the three way fight (hence there are many aspects of his analysis that I cannot cover here, such as his critique of Brahmanist metaphysics and ethics).[2] Though the terms may not directly translate, given differences between the North American and the Indian contexts, there are many features of Ajith's analysis that resemble a three way fight approach. The spirit of his critique is encapsulated in the epigraph to *Critiquing Brahmanism*, Dr. B. R. Ambedkar's observation, "Brahmanism and Capitalism, these two are the real enemies of the workers." Brahmanism, according to Ajith, undergirds Indian ruling-class ideology, ranging from the Indian National Congress (INC) and the parliamentarian left which has attempted to capture the Gandhi-Nehru legacy, to the Hindutva far right. Ajith's critique has clear parallels with the three way fight, though the two have developed independently of each other. I have argued, from the latter perspective, that in North America, both liberalism and far-right movements accept the basic coordinates of settler colonialism. Despite instituting some protections for minority rights, liberalism's ideology generally upholds the tenet that "we [*sic*] are a nation of immigrants," which occludes the ongoing legacy of Indigenous dispossession and slavery, while far-right movements tend to demand the re-entrenchment of settler capitalism's specific forms of oppression and exploitation on terms more conducive to white settlers. Hence the following parallel: fascism cannot be permanently defeated until the conditions which give rise to it are overthrown: capitalism and settler-colonialism in North America; capitalism and Brahmanism in India. Therefore, those interested in the three way fight and a thoroughgoing revolutionary criticism of Brahmanism will find much of interest in *Critiquing Brahmanism*.

Ajith contends that Brahmanism forms the hegemonic center of the comprador-bureaucratic bourgeoisie that emerged under and through colonialism and assumed power in postcolonial India. As a religious and cultural system, Brahmanism has undergone numerous changes over time, sometimes shaped by ruling class interests and at other times under pressure exerted by particular oppressed castes—for example, the *Shudra* (menial workers) and *Avarna* ("untouchables," *Adivasi*, and other castes)—though throughout these changes its caste system and support for patriarchal oppression have remained (11–12). Brahmanism is able to play its ideological and hegemonic role due to a degree of cultural and religious flexibility; "it allows space for some of the beliefs, deities, customs" of assimilated peoples to be accommodated, but by integrating them at "lesser levels in its own theology, pantheon and ethics. The whole process allows Brahmanism to appear as quite tolerant, even while it firmly consolidates its hegemony" and nurtures racism (8). Ajith surveys previous critics of Brahmanism: some have conflated it with Hinduism (while some currents of Hinduism are anti-Brahmanist, and thus it remains "possible and necessary" to differentiate between them); some, such as the aforementioned Ambedkar, did not integrate their critique with anticolonialism and anti-imperialism; more recently, the parliamentarian left foreclosed a radical critique of Brahmanism by positioning itself as the true defender of the Gandhi-Nehru legacy. By contrast, Ajith argues that social revolution and emancipation require "a wholesale attack on Brahmanism; an attack that aims at annihilating it at the ideological, political, social, cultural, psychological and economic levels" (24).

The hegemonic role of Brahmanism in contemporary India is inseparable from the history of colonialism. Despite the fact that Brahmanism, and its core philosophy of *Advaita* (characterized as non-dual thought or absolute monism), enjoyed limited hegemonic success prior to colonization, it was elevated to "the foremost achievement of South Asian philosophy and the world outlook of Hinduism" through colonial Orientalism (9). For example, nineteenth-century German philosophers took *Advaita* as one mystical progenitor of Western philosophy, albeit one that they thought either needed to be subsumed and explained through the rational (and Christian) religion of the

German idealists or proffered as a vitalistic counterpoint to the rigidity of Kantian ethics, as in Schopenhauer.

Of course, in India, Brahmanism's caste system facilitated British colonial rule. Marx predicted that British rule and the development of industry "will dissolve the hereditary divisions of labour, upon which rest the Indian castes, those decisive impediments to Indian progress and Indian power," which would facilitate the creation of the material conditions necessary for social revolution.[5] Contrary to Marx, Ajith observes that the development of capitalism in the colonies did not follow the path of the Western metropoles. Instead, capitalism in India "served both imperialism and feudalism" (12). The comprador-bureaucrat bourgeoisie that assumed power in post-Independence India emerged from upper castes (*Brahmin, Kshatriya, and Vaishya*) supported by elements of Jain, Christian, and Muslim upper castes. As a set of religious, philosophical, and cultural beliefs and values, Brahmanism functions as the basis of ruling-class ideology. It provided an ideological link between the emerging new bourgeoisie and the feudal classes that persisted through the colonial period and beyond; it provides, for both the liberal project of the INC and Hindutva nationalists and fascists, continuity between pre-colonial and post-Independence India. For Gandhi and the INC, Brahmanism offered a vision of "unity in diversity," accommodating some concerns of lower castes and ethnic minorities, while at the same time producing an imagined Indian nation existing from antiquity, seeking to regain "its assumed world status and glory through anti-colonial struggle" (15). Ajith observes that Gandhi was instrumental in weaving together modern bourgeois elements of nationalism and economic development into "Brahmanic fabric with the liberal deployment of Hindu symbols" (15).

This imagined India has served an entirely different purpose for the Hindutva far right (including the prominent Rashtriya Swayamsevak Sangh and Bharatiya Janata Party), which has pursued an "explicitly Brahmanist, North Indian version of Vaisihnavite Hinduism" that steamrolls distinct belief systems within Hinduism as well as the differences in Hindu practice and worship, including differences between "Hindu castes living in the same cultural region" (6). Ajith argues that Brahmanism has played an important role in reshaping the hegemonic consensus around Hindutva nationalism. Because the Hindutva movement, historically speaking, kept away from the struggle against British colonialism, Brahmanism has played an important role in burnishing the movement's anticolonial credentials.

The far right has also reshaped Indian nationalism around the collective rebirth of an imagined India of antiquity and inflated scientific advancement — Hindutva ideologists assert, for example, that "ancient Hindus developed plastic surgery and flew airplanes"[4] — brought to ruin by "Muslim invasion" (78). Just as Ajith emphasizes the Orientalist and colonial roots of the modern elevation of Brahmanism, he dedicates an entire chapter to demonstrating that India's scientific decline was a product of European colonialism and Brahmanism, which share scorn for the scientific heritage of "local knowledge systems and practices" — the former in order to further the colonial project, while the latter drew a stark division between manual and mental labor, severing local knowledges and practices from theory (77–87). Finally, Hindutva reshapes the idea of "unity in diversity" around Hindu nationalism and the re-entrenchment of caste oppression.

We are now in a position to compare Ajith's critique of Brahmanism and capitalism to the three way fight, which holds, first, that the struggle against fascism cannot be collapsed into the broader struggle against capitalism, even though capitalism is one condition which gives rise to and enables far-right movements; and second, that militant antifascism rejects the idea that reestablishing liberal or democratic norms constitutes a victory against far-right movements. Ajith draws a crucial distinction between Brahmanism and capitalism, which cannot be reduced to a relation of superstructure and base (as a more orthodox Marxist approach might). Thus, we cannot readily assume that so-called superstructures implemented in exploitative societies immediately dissipate under the pressures of successful proletarian revolutions. Class, he observes, is mediated by other social relations, such as "caste, gender, ethnicity, regionality, nationality and religious community ... each of these have their specific dynamic that impinges on that of class" (55). Though Brahmanism plays an important hegemonic role under the present system of capitalism in India, Ajith argues that overthrowing present relations of exploitation is not sufficient to "eliminate all grounds for another adaptive adjustment of Brahmanism" (24). He concludes that as long as remnants of caste and patriarchy exist, Brahmanism will remain a rallying point for reaction.

In terms of the three way fight, Ajith identifies Brahmanism as the line of adjacency between the comprador-bureaucrat bourgeoisie aligned with the INC and that of the Brahmanic Hindutva far right. Though the latter departs from the supposed secular democratic norms of the former, Brahmanism and capitalism enable both. Therefore, it is not enough to push for a return to these norms—from the Brahmanic Hindutva "unity in diversity," which *subsumes* diversity into Hindu nationalism, to a more liberal emphasis on diversity. Hence Ajith's critique of the revisionist Communist Party of India (Marxist): by positing itself as the true defender of the Gandhi-Nehru legacy, it is unable to develop a thoroughgoing critique of Brahmanism. Instead, its emphasis on "diversity" as opposed to Hindutva "unity" remains "firmly placed in a common frame set up by Brahmanism. This causes a blunting of the ideological, political attack on Brahmanic Hindu fascism. Worse, it traps many who wish to join this struggle in a pretence, a superficial opposition, allowing the ruling classes to contain it within safe channels" (54).

Finally, one other feature ought to give us pause In North America, the far right often frames at least part of its program around the explicit rejection of tolerance. If Ajith is correct that Brahmanic Hindu fascism builds hegemony and retains its position through assimilation and the outward appearance of accommodation or toleration, then we must use that insight to fight back against international points of contact and possible ideological exchange between different forms of far-right organizing. *Critiquing Brahmanism*, then, is an important tool for militant antifascists.

NOTES

1. Don Hamerquist et al., *Confronting Fascism: Discussion Documents for a Militant Movement*, 2nd edition (Montreal: Kersplebedeb, 2017), 28.

2. K. Murali (Ajith), *Critiquing Brahmanism: A Collection of Essays* (Paris: Foreign Languages Press, 2020).

3. Karl Marx, "The Future Results of the British Rule in India" in *Surveys from Exile: Political Writings*, vol. 2, ed. David Fernbach (London: Penguin, 173), 323.

4. Walden Bello, *Counterrevolution: The Global Rise of the Far Right* (Black Point, Nova Scotia: Fernwood, 2019), 77.

8. Reconstructing a Communist Antifascist History

T. Derbent is a communist theorist of military strategy, whose research and writing focus on the influence of the nineteenth-century Prussian general Carl von Clausewitz's theories on revolutionary thought. His *Categories of Revolutionary Military Policy* (Kersplebedeb, 2006) already circulates within militant circles due to its concise taxonomy of different types of revolutionary struggle. Soon two other works will join that work and the present volume [*German Communist Resistance 1933-1945*] in English translation, to be published by Foreign Languages Press: *Clausewitz et la guerre populaire* (2004) and *De Foucault aux Brigades rouges: misère du retournement de la formule de Clausewitz* (2018).[1]

The German Communist Resistance 1933–1945 is to some degree an outlier in Derbent's work, if not a detour. It was first published in 2008 and then reprinted in 2012 with the addition of two interviews with the author as appendices. In those interviews, he explains how he came to discover unpublished archival materials documenting widespread clandestine resistance on the part of the German Communist Party (KPD). After failing to persuade others to follow up on this line of research, Derbent finally decided to take on the project himself, thus correcting a

---

Originally part of the preface to T. Derbent's *German Communist Resistance 1933–1945*, published by Foreign Languages Press (2021).

glaring historical omission in Western historiography—including antifascist historiography, no less.

In broad outline, the received history of Nazi Germany holds that Nazi repression of socialist and communist opposition was swift. The main Communist Party leaders were arrested and detained in concentration camps while many thousands of cadres went into exile to fight fascism from abroad. A viable resistance only begins in the late 1930s, organized by anti-Hitler factions of the bourgeoisie and aristocracy (the Kreisau Circle or their "heirs," the conspirators who carried out an assassination attempt on Hitler on July 20, 1944) or among small networks of heroic dissidents, such as the White Rose group (whose best-known members are Hans and Sophie Scholl). Communist resistance is not entirely omitted from this received history, but it is said to re-enter near the end of the war and is grouped with socialist and Christian resistance. However, grouping these forms of resistance together is, in Derbent's terms, a "sham": Christian and socialist resistance was carried out by individuals or small networks; by comparison, only the communist resistance embraced all possible forms of struggle (propaganda, sabotage, guerrilla warfare, espionage, union struggle, etc.). It is the only one to have fought from the first to the last day of the Third Reich, and to have extended its action to the whole of Germany (even in the camps and in the army). Finally, it is the only one to have really weakened the Nazi war machine. (96)

Furthermore, although antifascist historiography acknowledges the role that the KPD played in numerous antifascist organizations, such as *Antifaschistische Aktion*, the discussion typically ends where Derbent's account takes off, with the Nazi suppression of the Communist Party in 1933. While clandestine work lacks the organizing capacity that open resistance has available to it, that does not nullify its impacts. The reader notes a certain amount of repetition as repression fails to stop resistance: KPD organizations carry out clandestine action, they are dismantled by the Gestapo, dozens if not hundreds of militants are rounded up and imprisoned or executed, the organizations are reconstituted and return to action. In the midst of this repression, the communist resistance carried out propaganda campaigns, supported strikes and sabotage of the war industry, and organized resistance in the army and in concentration camps. Derbent also catalogues the work of communists in exile, in the Spanish Civil War and in various occupied countries.

Derbent's short intervention is admittedly not exhaustive; it only aims to provide an overview of the scope and importance of communist resistance. By focusing almost exclusively on the KPD, he shows that the practice of the communist resistance followed a remarkably consistent clandestine policy of opposition to Nazism, even as the political line of the Soviet Union and Comintern shifted over time. Indeed, Derbent presents some evidence that the Soviet-aligned militants of the KPD continued to carry out clandestine actions against the Nazis during the period of the non-aggression pact between Germany and the Soviet Union. I would conclude on this basis that when Derbent contends that German communist resistance maintained a continuous opposition to Nazism, this continuity was one of military policy rather than political policy, a continuity that is perhaps legible only when we focus, as Derbent's analysis frequently does, on the former rather than the latter. At the same time, it is worth noting that in *Categories of Revolutionary Military Policy*, Derbent argues that European communist parties failed to defeat Nazi invasion due to their organization as "primarily legal parties supplemented by clandestine military structures"; on his account, they were more effective when improvising practices of protracted people's war.[2] It would have been interesting to see this argument integrated within *The German Communist Resistance*.

In any case, the clandestine resistance he describes dwarfs that of the individuals and groups typically celebrated in popular Western historiography; today's reader will be surprised to discover the quantity of munitions and planes rendered inoperable by communist sabotage.[3] These historical omissions are the

105

result of a Western, anti-communist political consensus, which continues to treat communism and fascism as two sides of the same totalitarian coin. And yet, today just as yesterday, supposedly liberal and progressive—but anticommunist—blocs attempt to make peace with far-right and fascistic political tendencies in order to shore up capitalist hegemony.

♧⤳⤶♧

Antifascist historiography, at least in the English-speaking world, tends to date the emergence of modern militant antifascism around 1946, with the formation of the 43 Group in England.[4] The 43 Group, which was comprised mainly, but not exclusively, of Jewish veterans of World War II, used physical confrontation to break up public meetings and rallies of a variety of fascist groups. They used direct action to undermine fascist organizing because the typical liberal mechanisms of social mediation—a combination of the inculcation of liberal norms, the so-called marketplace of ideas, and law enforcement—do not. Indeed, liberal norms and legislation tend to permit far-right or fascist organizing on the basis of freedom of speech and association while police are sympathetic to far-right groups for a variety of reasons, reasons we will return to below. In light of the failures of liberal mechanisms to halt fascist organizing, the 43 Group carried out its actions as a form of "communal defense."[5] M. Testa summarizes this period of antifascist struggle in terms which are contemporary enough: "militant anti-fascists found themselves in a 'three-cornered fight' against both fascists and the police ... anti-fascists were statistically three times more likely to be arrested than fascists. The police justified this by interpreting anti-fascist activity as aggressive and thus, wittingly or not, acted as stewards for fascist meetings to 'preserve the peace'."[6] While antisemitism, and even fascist sympathies, among law enforcement certainly played a part in police actions, "the police were never convinced that the Group was apolitical and not secretly communist. Consequently, like their communist allies, the anti-fascist ex-servicemen were seen as radical agitators desperate to overturn the status quo."[7]

If the modern history of militant antifascism typically takes the 43 Group as its point of departure, it is because the Group took on the three way fight against both system-oppositional far-right and fascist groups and law enforcement (or more broadly, the repressive apparatus of bourgeois class rule). This three way fight would be familiar to antifascists out in the streets of North America (and elsewhere) over the last five years, but the events of the last year during the pandemic show that the political coordinates of struggle are both volatile and subject to rapid change. In my view, Derbent offers us a window into a particularly important moment—the struggle between the KPD and the German Social Democratic Party (SPD) during the rise of the Nazi Party—from a theoretically fruitful angle.

There is a temptation when revisiting the failures of the KPD and SPD as the Nazis ascended to political power to re-litigate their ideological debates in order to settle political scores. It may be impossible not to belie one's commitments when analyzing these failures. Derbent, for his part, takes a critical approach to the KPD's political line by contextualizing it via social antagonism. He writes:

> The communist leadership believed that the antifascist struggle involved the elimination of social-democratic influence in the proletariat, because this influence distanced the class from a genuine antifascist and anti-capitalist struggle. This analysis had two premises. The first—erroneous—was the widespread idea at the time that the Nazi movement would not withstand the test of power, that it would crack both because of the workers' opposition and because of its internal contradictions. But the second premise of the KPD's analysis was correct: the will to fight Hitlerism was totally lacking in social democracy. The SPD's legalism led it to fight the communists rather than the Nazis. (27)

On this basis, Derbent analyzes two related political lines held by the KPD in the run up to the Nazis taking power in 1933: first, the "third period" policy that held that socialists were "social fascists," that is, that social democrats functioned as a moderate wing of fascism, allied with the bourgeoisie against communism; and second, the two-front struggle of the "united front at the base," which consisted of fighting socialist leadership and organizations while building alliances with the SPD rank and file.

We will begin with the latter. As Derbent notes, the united front at the base policy resulted in an ambivalent political position: "The KPD could do or not do anything; it served 'objectively' either the Social Democrats or the Nazis" (28). It led, infamously, to the KPD's participation in a Nazi-inspired referendum against the social-democratic government in Prussia in 1931. Derbent hints at the internal struggles within the KPD when deciding these policies, but does not underline the policies that resulted in the failures of the united front at the base. Here, I find Nicos Poulantzas's verdict persuasive: the KPD relied on "electoral struggle as the favoured form of 'mass action'."[8] At the same time, he adduces evidence that the KPD failed to set up united front organizations which could cement alliances between communists and the rank and file of the social democrats.[9]

Part of the failure of the united front at the base policy can be placed on the line that socialists were social fascists. Derbent departs from the typical reception of this part of the third period line. Some critics relegate the third period to the Stalinization of the Comintern, where "Moscow politics often influenced continental anti-fascist strategy more than Italian or German realities"—but this emphasizes external factors over contradictions internal to these "German realities."[10] By contrast, Derbent argues that the social fascist line was validated by the fact that social democrats repeatedly used the repressive state apparatus to quell communist organizing. The failure of the KPD and the SPD to align against the Nazis was not merely ideological, but was also driven by antagonism between communist insurrectionism and the SPD, which presided at the helm of the repressive state apparatus. The socialist adherence to legalism, which brought repressive state power to bear on communist organizing, also put the leadership of the SPD at odds with cadre on the ground who sought a more militant line for the Iron Front, the SPD's antifascist fighting organization.[11] Yet communists failed to seize the opportunity. As Poulantzas writes:

> As far as the line itself is concerned, the inclusive des-
> ignation of social democracy and the social-democratic
> trade unions as social fascist and as the main enemy,
> bore heavy responsibility for the failure of the united
> front. This was not so much because of the refusal of
> all contact between the leaderships, and even between
> the secondary ranks; *it was particularly because of the
> policy toward the social-democratic masses, considered
> "lost" as long as they were under the influence of social
> democracy* … Even apart from the fact that the KPD's
> main activity was still directed against social democ-
> racy, this activity was conceived of as a struggle be-
> tween "organizations," not as mass struggle on a mass
> line.[12] (my emphasis)

Though the KPD sought to form a united front with social-democratic workers in principle, they failed to translate this into practice. The "social fascist" label, in my view, is a symbol of this failure to build a mass struggle around a united front, and it lives on as an inflammatory epithet, largely doing the same work today. Nonetheless, what I have tried to excavate, via Derbent, is how, at the time, this misguided terminology reflected—in a partial way—realities on the ground. While socialists and communists had a common enemy, organizationally they occupied structurally different social positions: one commanded state power and the other's insurrectionary strategy was repeatedly quashed by the repressive state apparatus. But the KPD also failed to focus on the struggle beyond these organizational parameters. We must underline this kernel of truth while dispensing with the husk, which belies how communists underestimated the strength of emerging threat of fascism.

NOTES

1. T. Derbent, *The German Communist Resistance 1933–1945*. (Paris: Foreign Languages Press, 2021), 1–18. Derbent's *Clausewitz and the People's War, and Other Politico-Military Essays* will be published by Foreign Languages Press in 2024.

2. T. Derbent, *Categories of Revolutionary Military Policy* (Montreal: Kersplebedeb, 2006), 5.

3. See Derbent, *The German Communist Resistance*, 89–90.

4. See, for example, Mark Bray, *Antifa: The Anti-Fascist Handbook* (New York: Melville House, 2017), 39 ff.

5. This phrasing is from one of the Group's pamphlets, quoted in Daniel Sonabend, *We Fight Fascists: The 43 Group and Their Forgotten Battle for Post-war Britain* (London: Verso, 2019), 72.

6. M. Testa, *Militant Anti-fascism: A Hundred Years of Resistance* (Oakland: AK Press, 2015), 150.

7. Sonabend, *We Fight Fascists*, 119.

8. Nicos Poulantzas, *Fascism and Dictatorship: The Third International and the Problem of Fascism*, trans. Judith White (London: Verso, 1979), 184.

9. Poulantzas, *Fascism and Dictatorship*, 182.

10. Bray, *Antifa*, 20.

11. Bray, *Antifa*, 23–24.

12. Poulantzas, *Fascism and Dictatorship*, 182.

9. Where Do We Go Next?
A Review of Shane Burley's *Why We Fight*

When it was published in 2017, Shane Burley's *Fascism Today: What It Is and How to End It* was among a spate of books coming from the militant antifascist tradition that focused on outlining and combating the contemporary threat of fascism. Though his research began before the events surrounding the 2016 U.S. presidential campaign, it was given new impetus and urgency with the public emergence of the Alt Right as a political force and the election of Donald Trump as president. Burley's book stands out for melding the concerns of Mark Bray's *Antifa: The Antifascist Handbook* (2017) and the in-depth research on the far right that animates Matthew N. Lyons's *Insurgent Supremacists: The U.S. Far Right's Challenge to State and Empire* (2018). (Lyons also wrote the foreword for *Fascism Today*.) I cannot believe I'm about to deliver a retrospective evaluation of a book that is not yet five years old, but Lenin's apocryphal comment that "there are weeks where decades happen" resonates with many of us these days. *Fascism Today* remains, like Bray's and Lyons's respective contributions, one of the representative texts for understanding the concerns and aims of militant antifascism during the period of the 2016–2020 Trump presidency.

Published four years after *Fascism Today*, in 2021, Burley's *Why We Fight: Essays on Fascism, Resistance, and Surviving the Apocalypse* opens with a distinctly different mood,

Originally published on the *Three Way Fight* website, November 3, 2021.

with an introduction that ruminates on millenarian currents within fascist groups, climate apocalypse, and the possibilities opened up by an antifascist opposition—in a world of cyclical if not accelerating capitalist crises—to the ever-present threat of barbarism.[1] It's a mood that reflects the shifting terrain of militant antifascist struggle on the uncertain ground of the pandemic (having been compiled for publication, it seems, in Spring 2020), and it remains relevant in light of the more recent moment of liberal triumphalism (having electorally "defeated" so-called "Trumpism") and the theoretical and practical challenges posed by the reorganization of fascist and far-right movements. However, there is a sharp difference in mood between the Introduction and the first two thirds of the book, which has to do with how the book is organized. *Why We Fight* includes a selection of articles—some substantially revised—from 2017 to 2020, and it also contains a number of previously unpublished essays, several of which round out the end of the book.

THE FALL OF THE ALT RIGHT

As I read it, *Why We Fight* is loosely organized into three thematic sections. The first, from the chapter "Disunite the Right" to "The Fall of the Alt Right Came from Antifascism" (in other words, the first three chapters after the Introduction), covers the trajectory of the Alt Right, which one can glean through the chapter titles themselves. It is a direct sequel to Burley's analysis in *Fascism Today*. There, as I mentioned, he covers the rising threat of new fascist movements. Here, he chronicles the collapse of the Alt Right, which positioned itself for a time as the vanguard of the contemporary far right. This sequence demonstrates how pressure applied by militant antifascist organizing led to splits within far-right groups that had formed pragmatic but uneasy coalitions. The substance of Burley's argument is that the fight against fascism is not won by purely legal mechanisms (he contends that lawsuits can dismantle the financial or material infrastructure of particular far-right groups but not the broader movement as a whole) or debates in the so-called marketplace of ideas. He concludes:

> It is not the vague mysticism of public opinion or the spin from op-eds. What stops white nationalists is activists stopping white nationalists: stopping their project from functioning, from expanding, from making a difference. In this way, the antifascist movement — made up of church groups, student clubs, anarchists, and liberals — has prevented the Alt Right's infrastructure from self-replicating by throwing a monkey wrench into their machine. (59)

In other words, it was militant community-based organizing that outflanked the Alt Right's organizational efforts.

Each of what I view to be the three loosely thematic sections follows the same sequence: first, Burley sketches the ideological and organizational parameters of far-right activity, balancing how far-right groups elaborate these parameters and how they appear within a critical antifascist perspective, and then he concludes the sequence by examining how antifascists can fight back.

The first thematic section, then, shows how antifascist organizing can splinter far-right coalitions. As Burley notes throughout, fascism seeks to make the implicit hierarchies of social oppression explicit; for example, the United States as a settler-colonial society has a long and ongoing history of heteropatriarchy, anti-Black racism, and Indigenous dispossession, and fascist movements seek to re-entrench these social hierarchies to their own social, economic, and political advantage. In the chapter "Disunite the Right," Burley argues that coalitions between the Alt Right and the Alt Lite fractured over just how much of the implicit was to be made explicit. The Alt Right is a white identitarian movement which seeks to transform the

United States into an explicitly white ethnostate; "the Alt Right's principles ... all flow downstream from identity" (48). The Alt Lite, as the name implies, attempts to present a more palatable version of far-right ideology, which it presents as a kind of right-wing "civic nationalism": it "tempers its ideas about race yet still utilizes national chauvinism, protectionism, and isolationism" (40). As antifascist pressure mounted against their coalitions, the alliance between the two groupings fractured. The Alt Right entered coalitions with more explicitly fascist groups and was sidelined by broad antifascist counter-organizing after Charlottesville, while the Alt Lite—which, Burley contends, has a much bigger stake in protecting its social media grift, and hence is particularly responsive to pressures of no-platforming or de-platforming—was forced to distance itself from the more explicitly fascist subcultures of the far right. The fall of the Alt Right did not dismantle the danger of fascism and the far right, but it offers a lesson about how to apply pressure to undermine their often tenuous coalitions.

METAPOLITICS

The second thematic section, from "25 Theses on Fascism" to "How Racists Dream," covers a variety of organizational, cultural, and "metapolitical" aspects of far-right and fascist movements. The chapter "A History of Violence" examines how incidents of supposedly "lone wolf" violence are primed within far-right circles, sometimes implicitly by their rhetoric and behavior, sometimes explicitly, as in the case of Louis Beam's influential theory of "leaderless resistance" (laid out in an essay of the same name). Other chapters focus on far-right metapolitics, which attempts to shift the political and intellectual culture of society, pulling it rightwards, to make fascist ideas more palatable and mainstream. "How Racists Dream" covers how far-right publishing houses have attempted to lend fascist ideas an intellectual veneer. The essay "Contested Space" shows how antifascists have attempted to "go where they go" by contesting specific subcultural spaces, including music scenes (many of us remember how punks fought neo-nazis out of that scene decades ago; Burley here covers folk and metal), sports (soccer and gyms), "northern traditions" (heathenry), and self-defense clubs. As Burley notes, "when someone is inside of a subculture, or an organization with subcultural agency in particular, they have more power than they would have individually in the shifting ether of mass politics" (131). It would have been interesting had he followed up on this observation by assessing whether certain forms of far-right metapolitics have drifted toward subcultures rather than mass organizing because they have been outflanked by antifascists in street-level organizing, since one would presume that the more esoteric their references become, the more they are potentially sidelined within even far-right social ecologies, let alone mass organizing efforts. Nordic symbolism and references to Julius Evola might not carry the same overt and widely recognized historical baggage as references to Nazism or Mussolini, but they also aren't as readily recognizable as the rhetoric and symbols of right-wing "civic nationalism" evinced by the Patriot movement and the Alt Lite.

SELF-HELP AND SUPREMACISM

The third thematic section, from "Introduction to Armageddon" to the end of the book, is defined not so much by a common theme as by a common scope. There are essays on a wide variety of topics: climate catastrophe, blackface and white identity, a recent history of far-right violence, Rojava and anarchist internationalism, antisemitism, and male supremacist subcultures. There is also a current of autobiographical self-reflection that runs through several essays, but a reconstruction of this aspect is beyond the scope of this review.

Here I will look at the final essay of the book, "Chasing the Black Sun," which examines male supremacist fascism. On the face of it, male supremacist groups which lack an unambiguous racial bar don't appear as fascist according to many definitions of the term, though they would still be categorized as far right. Burley argues that the Wolves of Vinland and Operation Werewolf (both founded by Paul Waggener) are fascist. The Wolves of Vinland are well known to researchers of the far right, and Burley notes that within the far-right milieu their "fascist bonafides are unquestionable" (263). The present discussion will focus on Operation Werewolf (hereafter OPWW). Burley argues that OPWW sanitizes much of the white supremacist ideology which undergirds the Wolves of Vinland, which does not stop this "self-help business empire" from also acting as a Trojan horse for "venerating all of their [white nationalists'] key ideological impulses" (264).

In a way, OPWW is a combination of social-media marketing or branding and far-right movements. Its program is a smattering of self-help, pop psychology, financial advice, spirituality, and physical training. There's also a grift vibe, as Waggener markets himself as the "brand" or aesthetic of this kind of masculinity. But within that program is a vision of masculine domination and violence against a decadent and effeminate society. Many of its core programmatic components fall squarely within the parameters of fascism that Burley sketches in his "25 Theses on Fascism." As Burley argues in Thesis 25, fascism makes the implicit hierarchies in society explicit, and male supremacist movements explicitly and consciously embrace the patriarchal hierarchies of (in the case of North America) settler-colonial societies, which they perceive to be in crisis: "that men's role over women is deserved, natural, and based on what is lacking in women" (299). Furthermore, Waggener's groups stoke the idea that masculinity is based on an assertion of the will, including through violence. As noted in Thesis 17: "fascism seeks to sanctify violence, built directly into their [sic] conception of identity and a correctly hierarchical society" (66).

In Thesis 6, Burley contends that contemporary fascism "is largely built on metapolitics rather than explicit politics. Fascist projects attempt to influence culture, perspectives, and morality as precursors to politics" (62–63). Waggener presents himself, in a manner to be imitated, in an aggressive, hypermasculine style, but the aestheticization goes beyond his own personal brand, beyond the LARPing for which his groups are sometimes ridiculed, to aesthetic choices that embrace symbolism which has already been appropriated by Nazism and white supremacists. Thus this symbolism, which is esoteric enough to allow for plausible deniability, has already been reinterpreted in a way which venerates white supremacist ideology. The most obvious choice is Waggener's use of the Nordic Black Sun as a symbol of transformation (hence the title of the essay), but Burley also tracks the use of other examples. He demonstrates, at several points throughout the book, how both white supremacists and male supremacists have drawn on Julius Evola's traditionalist reinterpretation of "Kali Yuga" (one phase in the Vedic Cycle of Ages) as the contemporary age of decadence: "the current state of Kali Yuga is blamed for 'modern, liberated women,' Type II diabetes, and everything in between—all signs that we have lost our true path and an indicator that becoming an Operation Werewolf Operative can set you free" (271).

In addition, he contends that while the ideology of OPWW tones down the explicit white supremacism of the Wolves of Vinland by offering a vision of male supremacist, supposedly ethnopluralist nationalism for all peoples (in line with Burley's tenth thesis), white supremacism returns in the mythology peddled by Waggener. This mythology—including a seemingly eclectic collection of Nordic and Vedic symbols—is itself based on a belief that Europeans and much of Hindu South Asia share a common ancestry in "mythic Indo-European peoples," an idea that has "been part and parcel of white supremacist literature," and which "places a certain amount of white racial ownership over Hinduism" (269). Here Burley is especially effective in showing that male supremacists' symbolic choices draw their salience from associations with the broader far-right milieu.

Before concluding, Burley examines feminist approaches to masculinity, including the work of bell hooks and Nora Samaran, in order to suggest antifascist alternatives to male supremacism. Patriarchal concepts of masculinity are characterized by cultur-ally and historically specific values accorded to supposedly im-mutable natural or biological characteristics, which function to explain away relations of oppression that suffuse patriarchal so-cieties: hardness and immobility are contrasted with the "weak-nesses" of vulnerability, adaptability, and care. These charac-teristics are an ill-fitting ensemble for some men (Burley, in an autobiographical reflection, offers his father as an example). In the male supremacist worldview, this ill fit is explained away as a symptom of weakness, decadence, and effeminacy; masculin-ity is characterized as an open embrace of domination and vio-lence. An antifascist worldview offers a transvaluation of mas-culinity based on building relationships of reciprocity, care, and adaptability. As Burley writes, "if we see masculinity as a proper construct, a cluster of aspirations and traits, then we can recon-struct it the way we see fit—perhaps even beyond masculinity altogether and toward a different kind of person" (304).

CRITICISM I: BURLEY ON MARXISM

At its best, Burley's work distils the complicated and sometimes contradictory features of fascist movements while advocating for militant antifascism with rigor, clarity, and succinctness. However, there are numerous problems with Burley's engage-ment with revolutionary theory—and more specifically, with Marxist approaches to revolutionary theory—and the class composition of fascism.

Some problems involve oversimplification. His analysis of Marx's essay "On the Jewish Question" is one-sided, lacking the kind of nuance found in one of his secondary sources, Enzo Traverso's *The Jewish Question: History of a Marxist Debate* (241).[2] At one point, he shoehorns Mao's revolutionary strategy into a dichotomy between riot and strike, neither of which is an appropriate category for protracted people's war (181). To be fair, the reference to Mao is made in passing, and the discussion of Marx is a programmatic reading which is part of a broader case showing that orthodox leftist approaches to antisemitism are inadequate to the task (a point with which I generally agree).

The chapter "Introduction to Armageddon" contains a more substantial misrepresentation of Marxist theory in general and of Clara Zetkin's work in particular. Burley argues that in our contemporary situation—marked by climate catastrophe, population displacement, and increased economic precarity in advanced capitalist economies—traditional forms of organizing will fail to bring the necessary revolutionary changes that can stave off greater catastrophe. Specifically, he argues that strikes will fail to bring revolutionary change because a growing number of the dispossessed lack a direct relation to production, hence making them part of a growing lumpenproletariat:

> As automation, the "gig economy," and economic decline ravage communities that once relied on unionized factories, public employment, and a reliable safety net for stability, the ranks of the lumpenproletariat enlarge. Historically Marxists loathed the lumpenproletariat. Clara Zetkin suggested the "venal lumpens" were ripe for terrorism, a popular notion in Marxist circles that masses unable to sustain themselves through wage labor were personally bankrupt and strategically useless since they lacked the ability to strike. The unemployed, houseless, nomads, Indigenous communities existing outside the economy, subsistence farmers, bohemians, and a range of conflicting and intersecting identities could be labeled as "lumpen." (181)

There is a kernel of truth here surrounded by much exaggeration and misrepresentation. It is true that Marxists historically have had an ambivalent attitude toward the lumpenproletariat, which includes fractions that have played an important role in counter-revolutionary movements. It is also true that, in classical Marxist theory, too many disparate groups are categorized as lumpen and dismissed in overly moralistic terms. But the implication here goes far beyond these criticisms; Burley contends that Marxism has little to offer outside of "classical" industrial organizing.

The reference to Zetkin was the clue that led me to read this passage with more attention. Zetkin's position here isn't nearly as well known as Marx's analyses in *The Class Struggles in France: 1848–1850* and *The Eighteenth Brumaire* or Mao's analyses of class in China from the 1920s, which are more representative in discussions of the lumpenproletariat. Nor is her work a substitute for the discussions of Black liberation movements in the 1960s, which prompted a critical reconsideration of the orthodox Marxist position on the lumpenproletariat. So, the reference to her work, in the broader scheme of things, is unusual.[3]

Burley would presumably know Zetkin through her early essays on fascism, some of the earliest to examine fascism as it emerged. Indeed, the reference to "venal lumpens," as far as I can tell, is drawn from her essay "The Struggle against Fascism."[4] Knowing this, I assume that her comment isn't attacking the unemployed, vagabonds, refugees, and others. In context, she is arguing that antifascists must carry out ideological and political struggle among a variety of social strata: "Let us not forget that violent fascist gangs are not composed entirely of ruffians of war, mercenaries by choice, and venal lumpens who take pleasure in acts of terror."[5]

In this passage, I presume her audience would think not only of Italian *fascisti*, but also of the Freikorps (who are also discussed by Burley): right-wing paramilitaries who led the reaction against communist revolutionary struggle in Germany. She isn't arguing that the entire lumpenproletariat is "ripe for

WHERE DO WE GO NEXT?

terrorism." Nor does this passage support the remainder of Burley's argument that Marxists hold that the lumpenproletariat is strategically useless because they cannot strike. Instead, her contention is that fascism cannot be reduced to a violent lumpen movement, meaning that antifascist organizing must agitate among a variety of classes before they find common cause within the far right. Furthermore, while the organizations to which Zetkin belonged, the Communist International and KPD (*Kommunistische Partei Deutschlands*), failed to stem the tide of Nazism, it wasn't for want of organizing the unemployed. As Nicos Poulantzas observes, the KPD recruited "among the unemployed in enormous numbers after 1930. In 1932, only about 22 per cent of its members were actually in work."[6] I am unsure who would be representative of the position Burley criticizes — not being able to strike is not the relevant criterion for Marx or Mao—though I can imagine how it might apply to some proponents of syndicalism or social democracy.

CRITICISM II: FASCISM AND CLASS

In general, though, Burley's mishandling of the concept of the lumpenproletariat is part of a broader lack of clarity about class that runs throughout *Why We Fight*. As he notes in his second thesis on fascism, one of the conditions that enables fascist movements is the "destructive upheaval of class society" (61). In that same thesis, he argues that fascism does not require "a fixed demographic of finance capital," which I understand to be a critique and rejection of the orthodox (popular front) Marxist position, presented by Dimitrov in 1935 but also later adopted by the Black Panther Party. The BPP's line states: "Fascism is the open terroristic dictatorship of the most reactionary, most chauvinistic (racist) and the most imperialist elements of finance capital."[7] On this point Burley and I agree. However, I disagree with his vague and inconsistent definition of fascism as

121

a working-class movement. We could classify his descriptions into three conceptual clusters:

▶ Some characterize fascism as having a working-class base: "fascists employ the power of marginalized classes" (63); it recruits from "large segments of the working class" (67); the "white nationalist movement" is "known for its working class and rural base" (159).

▶ Others explain working-class collaboration with fascism or white supremacy as a protection of interests or privilege: "white supremacy is the autoimmune disease of the working class" (112); fascism is "a mass movement of working people turned against their own interests in a desperate bid to hold onto privilege" (148); "As crisis becomes the new normal, splits will form in the working class, with privileged groups fighting to maintain their menial comforts" (171).

▶ Finally, some passages upend his definition: "The Alt Right is white nationalism for the twenty-first century middle class male, and it then creates crossover spaces with Trump Republicans, civic nationalist types, anti-liberal libertarians, and so on" (78).

There are several problems with defining fascism as a working-class movement. First, supposedly common-sense terms like "elite," "middle class," and "working class" are too vague and imprecise, especially when applied to advanced capitalist societies such as the United States and Canada. Indeed, in common usage, these ostensibly class categories are also moral appraisals. Thus, even if it were true that fascism is a working-class movement, it would be necessary to offer a critical approach that challenges the biases of paternalistic liberals who view far-right politics as a backwards and atavistic relic of uneducated working-class and rural whites.

A militant antifascist perspective must adhere to more rigorous class categories to counter these biases and to counter far-right and antisemitic attempts to commandeer anti-elitist sentiment within a wide range of social movements. In my view, Marxist class categories—once they have been critically examined through prisms such as, but not limited to, race and gender—are far more specific than common-sense notions. The working class is, as Bromma notes, "a family of three separate classes": the proletariat, the worker elite (or, classically, the "labor aristocracy"), and the lumpenproletariat:[8]

▶ The proletariat, which makes up a majority of the working class around the globe, includes workers who fall into Engels's classic definition of the proletariat—"modern wage labourers who, having no means of production of their own, are reduced to selling their labour-power in order to live" (a description of work that is not exclusive to manufacturing)—but it can also include workers involved in unwaged labor (such as housework) and work that is done outside the formal economy, as well as the unemployed. The proletariat lives at or near the level of bare subsistence.

▶ The lumpenproletariat is a small part of the working class that exists outside of any direct relation to legal production and distribution—though *who* is included in the lumpenproletariat remains subject to controversy. *Contra* Burley, while there are elements of the unemployed, the houseless, or Indigenous peoples who fall into the lumpenproletariat, each such group as a whole is not lumpen: the unemployed are part of the proletariat, as would be working houseless people; Indigenous peoples are colonized nations containing a variety of classes. More typically, especially in discussions of fascism, the lumpen of concern are white supremacist gangs, ex-soldiers, and professional mercenaries.

▶ The worker elite exists between the bourgeoisie and proletariat; it is more accurately described as part of the "middle class." Bromma contends that the worker elite cannot be distinguished as skilled versus un-skilled labor nor merely by a certain level of income. Instead, holistically speaking, the worker elite re-ceives (1) a privileged standard of living (in terms of both income and social benefits), and (2) some degree of access to the political system; (3) it is positioned on the side of power in relation to existing fault lines of social struggle (for example, in the U.S., typically the worker elite is white when we consider racial fault lines, male when it comes to gender, and it has thrown their support behind American imperialism, etc.); and (4) it receives systemic and durable privileges, built into the social fabric.[9]

With these definitions in mind, the class composition of fascism will become more clear (with the caveat that there remains some degree of simplification in this presentation). We must observe, first, that the presence of some elements of a given class does not mean that a particular class *drives* insurgent far-right move-ments. That there are lumpen elements in an ideology that ven-erates violence is beyond controversy. The assumption that in order to ascend to power there must be some degree of collabo-ration between fascist movements and fractions of the bourgeoi-sie contributes to our understanding of how fascist movements might exploit factionalism within the bourgeoisie. However, in my view, neither of these factors explain the class character and potential mass base of insurgent far-right and fascist movements.

Revisiting Burley's analyses, then, our first question is: which remaining section of the working class offers a potential mass base for fascism? According to the definitions I proposed above, his references to the "working class" refer more specifically to the worker elite. As I have already noted, the presence of white proletarians doesn't mean that fascism is a proletarian movement. If we maintain definitions of class along the lines suggested by Bromma, meaning that the majority of proletarians in North America are women and/or workers of color, it is generally recognized that these groups are the targets of far-right violence, not its social base. Thus, while it is imprecise to categorize fascism as drawing on "marginalized classes," Burley would be correct to observe that those elements of the worker elite that join far-right movements do so to defend their social and class privileges, and this brings them into conflict with other parts of the working classes.

There is one more twist, however. In *The Anatomy of Fascism*, liberal historian Robert Paxton examines the class composition of fascist movements and concludes that working-class participation was proportionally lower than other sections of society, because "those already deeply engaged, from generation to generation, in the rich subculture of socialism, with its clubs, newspapers, unions, and rallies, were simply not available for another loyalty."[10] Now, the North American worker elite is hardly engaged with a "rich subculture of socialism," but some sections of this class do have unions. Without downplaying how worker elites and their unions and organizations have historically participated in preserving "social peace" within capitalism — in Burley's terms, preserving the "implicit" social and economic hierarchies in class society — we could also expect that the participation of worker elites in unions or cultures of solidarity offers a point of resistance against the far-right's explicit *desiderata*. Nonetheless, we must also acknowledge the potential mass base available through the worker elite that either lack unions or is openly anti-union.

Burley's most succinct encapsulation of twenty-first century fascism is his identification of the "middle-class" character of its momentary "vanguard" at the time, the Alt Right (78). In my view, it is disaffected elements of both the worker elite and the petty bourgeoisie—two factions of this "middle class"—that are driving contemporary far-right movements; they play a role in ideological leadership and the potential mass base. The leading figures of the Alt Right, for example, not only pursued post-secondary education but also adopted metapolitical strategies and arguments from the European New Right. Groups associated with the white identitarian movement sought—and still seek—to recruit members on college campuses and universities. As for the potential mass base, according to Robert A. Pape's analysis of 377 people arrested on charges related to the January 6 Capitol putsch, 44 percent were either business owners or white-collar workers. (We should be circumspect with this data, however; according to Pape, 87 percent of those arrested were unaffiliated with far-right groups.)[11]

In classical Marxist theory, the petty bourgeoisie was fated to disappear into the proletariat. As Marx and Engels argue in *The Communist Manifesto*, small capitalists or the petty bourgeoisie sink into the proletariat "because their diminutive capital does not suffice for the scale on which Modern Industry is carried." This "classical" statement has been used to justify lumping various classes under the rubric of the working class, since, the logic goes, Marx and Engels predicted the disappearance of the petty bourgeoisie more than one hundred and fifty years ago, so by now one must be either bourgeois or proletarian (the one percent or the ninety-nine percent, as one leftist argot has it). By contrast, as Rosa Luxemburg shows, the disappearance of the petty bourgeoisie does not proceed in a linear fashion; the fate of the petty bourgeoisie is subject to contradictions and thus must be handled dialectically. Hence, small capitalists serve a concrete role in capitalist development: "they initiate new methods of production in well-established branches of industry; they are instrumental in the creation of new branches of production not yet exploited by the big capitalist."[12] The small capitalist exists in the interstices of big capital until their diminutive capital no longer suffices to stay competitive within an increasing scale of production, and this cycle appears as "a periodic mowing down

WHERE DO WE GO NEXT?

of small enterprises, which rapidly grow up again, only to be mowed down once more by large industry."[13]

The petty bourgeoisie and the worker elite occupy different places within the capitalist mode of production. Like the worker elite, though, the North American petty bourgeoisie has typically allied with whiteness when confronted with antiracist struggle, just as it has allied with patriarchy when confronted with women's struggle. It has invested in American imperialism because American imperialism served its own interests. And the petty bourgeoisie, since it is composed of owners of capital, has received similar if not superior systemic and durable social privileges as the worker elite. Despite these differences, both classes occupy an especially unstable position in an economy governed by neoliberal policy and subject to crisis, which endangers their class status. And, despite their differences, these two classes adopt the same ideological maneuvers, presenting themselves as producers, patriots, citizens, or "the people," at the same time as they benefit from class, racial, and gender oppression, and — in settler-colonial societies such as ours — ongoing Indigenous dispossession. The far right's metapolitics, so aptly chronicled by Burley's analyses, attempts to modulate this ideological language around the explicit embrace of the implicit hierarchies that the middle classes — the *white* middle classes — have historically fortified.

CONCLUSION

The purpose of class analysis is to illuminate the potential social bases and class tendencies of far-right movements. I believe that this type of analysis can help antifascists glean insight into far-right organizational forms and their potential weaknesses. I do not believe that class categories should be mechanically and uncritically applied to these movements, or else we risk falling back into dogmatic positions similar to those advanced by orthodox Marxists or paternalistic liberals. We must not forget that fascist ideology—documented extensively throughout *Why We Fight*—has an appeal which, while it typically draws white supremacist racial color lines, is able to cut across class divisions and sometimes also across its presumed racial and gender lines.

Class analysis demands that we keep our perspective trained on systemic features of our society, including capitalist class domination. A three way fight approach must maintain a revolutionary, anticapitalist, egalitarian horizon. The ills of society are not, as liberals have it, merely attributable to bad actors and necessarily imperfect but reformable institutions; nor are they, as the far right would have it, the product of secret cabals (often expressed in antisemitic conspiracy theories). We must continue to build a revolutionary, antifascist theory and praxis that stops fascists in the streets and that also aims to overthrow the conditions which make fascism possible. Shane Burley's *Why We Fight* is an important contribution to answering the question: where do we go next?

NOTES

1. Shane Burley, *Why We Fight: Essays on Fascism, Resistance, and Surviving the Apocalypse* (Chico: AK Press, 2021).

2. Enzo Traverso, *The Jewish Question: History of a Marxist Debate* (Haymarket Books, 2019).

3. See also J. Sakai, *The "Dangerous Class" and Revolutionary Theory: Thoughts on the Making of the Lumpen/proletariat* (Montreal: Kersplebedeb, 2017).

4. Clara Zetkin, *Fighting Fascism: How to Struggle and How to Win*, ed. John Riddell and Mike Taber (Chicago: Haymarket Books, 2017).

5. Zetkin, *Fighting Fascism*, 60.

6. Nicos Poulantzas, *Fascism and Dictatorship: The Third International and the Problem of Fascism*, trans. Judith White (London: Verso, 1979), 181.

7. The Black Panther Party, "Call for a United Front against Fascism," in *The U.S. Antifascism Reader*, ed. Bill V. Mullen and Christopher Vials (London: Verso, 2020), 269. The Black Panther Party adds the parenthesis "(racist)" to Dimitrov's formulation.

8. Bromma, *The Worker Elite: Notes on the "Labor Aristocracy"* (Montreal: Kersplebedeb, 2014), 4.

9. Bromma, *The Worker Elite*, 19–21.

10. Robert O. Paxton, *The Anatomy of Fascism* (New York: Vintage, 2004), 50.

11. See Robert A. Pape and Chicago Project on Security and Threats, "Understanding American Domestic Terrorism: Mobilization Potential and Risk Factors of a New Threat Trajectory," Division of the Social Sciences, University of Chicago, April 6, 2021.

12. Rosa Luxemburg, *Reform or Revolution?* (Paris: Foreign Languages Press, 2020), 17.

13. Luxemburg, *Reform of Revolution?*, 18.

10. Revisiting
Antifascism Against Machismo

In 2019, Tammy Kovich published, under the pseudonym Petronella Lee, the short pamphlet *Anti-Fascism Against Machismo: Gender, Politics, and the Struggle Against Fascism.* Her essay is an important contribution to antifascist literature, which highlights how misogyny is a "fundamental pillar" of contemporary fascist movements while making a compelling argument that gender liberation must be "a non-negotiable component of anti-fascism" (70).

When it was first published, Kovich's reflections on militant antifascist organizing spoke to problems that many organizers had difficulty articulating. It is easy to dismiss critics who accuse antifascist groups of being *merely* angry, blocked-up white dudes looking for a fight, because plenty of our experiences show otherwise. Antifascism is not about the optics, and if critics, the police, and fascists are on the wrong track identifying who antifascists are, who wants to correct them? But dismissing characterizations from outright opponents does not bring clarity to another, more difficult problem. Stanislav Vysotsky points out in *American Antifa*, his auto-ethnographic study of two antifascist groups (in two different cities) conducted between 2002–2005 and 2007–2010, that there was gender parity in both groups, as well as a high representation of individuals who identify as

Originally published on the *Three Way Fight* website, September 30, 2023.

LGBTQ.[1] Even if we acknowledge that an increased participation in antifascist organizing after the very public rise of the Alt Right in 2016 shifted the demographics of antifascist groups, I would argue that they remained relatively closer in composition to Vysotsky's snapshots than the stereotyped, unsympathetic public impressions. However, the persistence of machismo in these circles becomes even more difficult to untangle. Hence my first review of *Antifascism Against Machismo* (published in January 2020, and included as Chapter 4 of this book) focuses on Kovich's critique of, and her proposals to overcome, machismo in antifascist organizing, and I believe her observations remain relevant today.[2]

Given the impact of the original pamphlet in antifascist circles, I greatly appreciate the publication of a new edition of Kovich's *Antifascism Against Machismo*, which collects previously published commentaries by activists Butch Lee (from 2019) and Veronica L. (from 2020), with a new introduction by poet and abolitionist El Jones.[3] By gathering these voices together, this new edition takes on an explicitly broader scope than the original, often shifting registers between a critique of the far right and of North American iterations of settler-colonial capitalism. *Antifascism Against Machismo* is a genuine discussion document, much like the multi-author text *Confronting Fascism* (also published by Kersplebedeb), opening new paths to militant organizing while challenging widely held or sometimes dogmatic assumptions shared on the left. As with any genuine discussion, not all questions are resolved, and thus we'll circle back to a few at the end of this review.

∿꧁꧂∾

The catalyst for the present review is Butch Lee's commentary on Kovich's essay. Lee is known for a handful of underground movement texts that work in and through an unorthodox Marxism-Leninism to develop a theory and praxis of revolutionary gender liberation; texts such as *Night-Vision: Illuminating War and Class on Neo-Colonial Terrain* (co-authored with Red Rover), *Jailbreak Out of History: The Re-Biography of Harriet Tubman and "The Evil of Female Loaferism,"* and *The Military Strategy of Women and Children.*[4] Her work has had an under-recognized influence on the three way fight approach, perhaps due to the fact that her analyses had not honed in on contemporary fascism and far-right movements. Until now.

From the start, Lee transgresses the narrow, pressing questions for antifascist work that animate Kovich's original analysis. Lee moves between recollections of her early (and by her own account naive) activism, the patriarchal structure of capitalism, and neo-colonialism, surveying the terrain that gives rise to contemporary fascism. As Lee recounts, the problem of fascism first emerged as an urgent political issue within the Black liberation movement in the 1960s, epitomized by the Black Panther Party's United Front Against Fascism conference in Oakland in July 1969. At the time, fascism was conceptualized as a form of widening and intensified political repression which nonetheless was "something not as different from but similar to 'Americanism' itself" (82). She suggests, without separating which is which, that analyses of the era "had both XL size insights and XL size misunderstandings"—but now, "fascism/antifascism alike, there's a new deal in the cards" (82–83).

Conventional leftist concepts of antifascism were cast in the late 1960s—not only when they draw from Black liberation movements but also when they characterize far-right movements based on clichés from what Lee calls the "second-wave fascism" of George Lincoln Rockwell and the American Nazi Party. System-loyal, "patriotic" groups that "fixated on anti-Black race hatred job one" (83). Groups which she characterizes as "tactically dangerous" (because of the threat of violence) but which were generally considered cosplaying outliers within the surrounding white racist American society. Theories of fascism that focus exclusively on state repression or dismiss street-level far-right movements as anachronistic sideshows completely miss the threat of contemporary fascism.

Contemporary, or what Lee calls "third-wave," fascism is qualitatively different from the second-wave fascism of the 1950s and 1960s. It is system-oppositional and prioritizes both racial oppression *and* gender oppression. In contrast to the patriotic sentiments of the George Lincoln Rockwells of the bygone days of Segregation, third-wave fascism was born out of "Vietnam defeats, forced integration, and man-abandoning feminism," and seeks to overthrow the U.S. government in order to reconstitute a white-settlerist, patriarchal society (86). And whereas second-wave fascism focused on anti-Black oppression, the new far right is "built heavily around woman-hating that joins their formative race hatred they are better known for" (90–91). Here, Lee commends Kovich for being "light years" ahead of conventional, mainstream accounts of far-right misogyny and misogynistic violence. First, Kovich shows that the "manosphere," an online subculture of misogynistic discourses, overlaps with and functions as a pipeline toward fascist recruitment. Second, she outlines a spectrum of forms of fascist sexism, from patriarchal fascism to misogynistic fascism. Finally, she catalogs how the far right now explicitly venerates violence against women. Lee concludes that supposedly individual or isolated attacks on women presage "targeting us eventually as an entire gender class" (87). (Though it risks being redundant, it is worth mentioning that for Lee those targeted for "gender class" violence under patriarchy include women, children, and LGBTQ+ communities.) She argues that women are "the first proletariat, the first conquered colony" of euro-capitalism, socially imprisoned and pressed into the labor of social reproduction (an argument made in more detail in her *The Military Strategy of Women and Children*). Fascism seeks to revive the patriarchal recolonization of women's bodies (101–103).

⟍⟋⟍⟋

Lee challenges a common but unexamined assumption among antifascists: that militant antifascism is engaged in a limited or temporary struggle for community self-defense against street-level organizing by far-right movements; when this threat passes, the immediate tactical necessity for militant antifascist organizing will dissipate, and the various individuals and groups who make up a local united front will return to other types of radical political work. Both Kovich and Veronica L. make observations along this line, and on this point they are no different than other authors such as Mark Bray, Shane Burley, or myself. Sometimes these observations take on a more critical edge, but generally the cycles of antifascist organizing seem inevitable. Lee would certainly be familiar with variations on this theme from earlier cycles of antifascist organizing as well; for example, during the decline of Anti-Racist Action. So there must be something to this final verse before Lee has "sung [her] song" (115).

In my view, Lee makes two arguments to challenge the idea that antifascist organizing is a limited form of political work. First, Lee argues that the sexism and misogyny expressed by fascists are a small part of a much larger, growing and explicit, mass shift toward white right reaction (104–105). In other words, the confrontation with the far right doesn't end in the streets. I think most militant antifascists would agree; indeed, we were critical of liberal antifascists when they decided to log off after Trump was deposed from power. However, I think Lee's argument draws its political force from a second, largely implicit, line of argument. She writes:

> What [Kovich] isn't afraid to explore, is that women
> should lead our fight against fascism. Draw our own
> wider strategies. Make our own diversely talented
> groups. Because fighting fascism is a woman-centered
> struggle for our lives now. Antifascism is crucially
> about gender as well as race. (87–88)

The idea that militant antifascists return to their other militant political projects when the immediate threat of far-right movements taking to the streets abates, rests on a number of unexamined assumptions. Most importantly, we tend to assume that the politics of antifascist work parallels the politics of our "home" political circles, whether those are Marxist or anarchist, whether parties, affinity groups, or reading groups. However, what if gender liberation is truly integrated as "a non-negotiable component of anti-fascism" as Kovich justly demands? If fighting fascism becomes "a woman-centered struggle"? What home political circle can match this commitment to gender liberation, when mainstream feminism is mired in liberalism, and when the history of militant and revolutionary movements carries so much patriarchal baggage? Lee challenges a widely held assumption about the dynamic of struggle in order to point to a new political possibility for women-centered antifascist work.[5]

≈∂≈

By way of conclusion, I would like to highlight two issues that suffuse the discussions in the new edition of *Antifascism Against Machismo*, concerning the differing concepts of fascism and settler colonialism evoked by the participants. These problems are partially sketched in Veronica L.'s contribution, and I would like to briefly revisit them here. First, none of the contributors puts a full definition of fascism on the table. Generally, the authors tend toward discussing fascist or far-right movements as types of white supremacy, but sometimes the discussion wavers. For example, near the conclusion of her essay, Kovich notes that "Black liberation and decolonial movements have either explicitly or implicitly been engaged in fighting against fascism for hundreds of years" (71). Such a claim, aside from the anachronism, confuses rather than clarifies the relationship between fascism and settler colonialism. It's worth noting that Lee, who touches on the historical legacy of Black liberation movements' antifascism while also sketching a sequence of historical waves of fascism, glosses Kovich's claim with a subtle but important caveat: "Black people and Indigenous peoples and many others had been fighting *something like* fascism here from the start"

(80, my emphasis). That something, of course, is white settler colonialism.

Through this discussion, a second problem emerges, when it becomes clear that the different participants in this intergenerational dialogue adhere to (at least) two different views of settler colonialism. Lee applies a Leninist anti-imperialist concept of colonialism to settler colonialism. Imperialism divides the world into oppressor nations and oppressed nations; settler colonialism differs from "classical" European colonialism (which maintained distance between the metropole and periphery) insofar as the colonies of settler-colonial states are internal colonies. According to this "old school" paradigm of settler-colonialism all internal oppressed nations have a right to self-determination, and as we have seen above, Lee argues that women are an "internal colony" analogous to the New Afrikan nation. Veronica adheres to a "new school" concept of settler colonialism (her and I are both writing within the Canadian settler-colonial context where this concept is current among activists), which draws its core distinction between settlers and Indigenous peoples, the latter having the right to national self-determination.

Neither concept of settler colonialism entirely satisfactorily resolves questions raised by anticolonial struggle, and I believe there are difficulties translating the political demands made by one into the political language of the other. On the one hand, the new school concept, focused on the settler/Indigenous binary, encounters difficulties "placing" the self-determination claims of a New Afrikan nation. On the other hand, Veronica questions the implications of an autonomous (white) women's movement's claim to "space" or land, a claim grounded in the old school concept, "in an anti-Black settler state that has from its beginning involved white women enforcing its hierarchies and advancing its settlements" (125–126). Indeed, if we widen the lens to a broader left's organizational initiatives, squatting, occupying, or building commons are not inherently emancipatory or anticolonial in the settler-colonial context. The point of this comparison is not to adjudicate between the two concepts of settler colonialism, but rather, as Veronica notes, to highlight the ongoing work that needs to be done — even in the seemingly unrelated context of gender liberation and antifascist struggle.

Antifascism Against Machismo raises pressing questions about antifascism, feminism, gender liberation, and settler colonialism, through a genuine wide-ranging discussion between its participants. It is required reading for those interested in new directions for advancing militant antifascist work.

NOTES

1. Stanislav Vysotsky, *American Antifa: The Tactics, Culture, and Practice of Militant Antifascism* (Routledge, 2020), 52–53.

2. *Three Way Fight* also published a review of the original pamphlet. See Matthew N. Lyons, "Review of 'Anti-Fascism Beyond Machismo' by Petronella Lee," *Three Way Fight*, October 17, 2019.

3. Tammy Kovich, *Antifascism Against Machismo*. With an introduction by El Jones and commentary by Butch Lee and Veronica L. (Montreal: Kersplebedeb, 2023).

4. Butch Lee and Red Rover, *Night-Vision: Illuminating War and Class on Neo-Colonial Terrain* (Montreal: Kersplebedeb, 2017); Butch Lee, *Jailbreak Out of History: The Re-Biography of Harriet Tubman and "The Evil of Female Loaferism"* (Montreal: Kersplebedeb, 2015); Butch Lee, *The Military Strategy of Women and Children* (Montreal: Kersplebedeb, 2003).

5. J. Sakai recounts, from a different angle, what Lee considered a missed opportunity from an earlier period of political struggle in *The Shape of Things to Come* (Montreal: Kersplebedeb, 2023), 359ff.

III. Emancipatory Community Self-Defense

11. Why Judith Butler Is Wrong About Militant Antifascism (2022)

1. THE TERRAIN OF NONVIOLENCE

Judith Butler is a prominent philosopher and public intellectual whose work has been formative in gender studies and critical theory. In October 2021, they published an essay in *The Guardian* which argues that "anti-gender [i.e. anti-trans and/or queerphobic] movements are not just reactionary but *fascist* trends." Butler is not the first to make this connection but is one of the most prominent public philosophers to have done so. They conclude the essay with the resounding call that "the time for anti-fascist solidarity is now."[1]

However, their call for solidarity must be balanced against their previous criticisms of militant antifascism found in their works "Protest, Violent and Nonviolent" (2017) and *The Force of Nonviolence* (2020). The former raises explicit criticisms of militant antifascism, which we will address below. The latter, which outlines the philosophical underpinnings for the arguments of "Protest, Violent and Nonviolent" in more depth, proceeds at a curious level of abstraction and distance from contemporary events. Butler mounts a defense of nonviolence against the rising threat of violence from "security, nationalism, and neofascism" from the right and, in a vague circumlocution, "those on the left who claim violence *alone* has the power to effect radical social and economic transformation," (my emphasis) as well as those who defend the use of a diversity of tactics.[2] Their analyses and hence critiques, however, focus almost exclusively on state violence. They never define what they mean by "neofascism," while their few references to fascism focus on historical cases. In "Protest, Violent and Nonviolent," they are reticent to treat contemporary system-oppositional far-right organizing as a legitimate threat. As for the left, Butler never names who specifically upholds the claim that "violence *alone*" can effect radical change. While they reference those on the left who justify some violent tactics, the book lacks any discussion of militant antifascism, diversity of tactics, or black blocs. The most specific reference is a footnote that cites a recent anthology edited by scott crow, *Setting Sights: Histories and Reflections on Community Armed Self-Defense*, as defending a "contrary view" to their own (14n11).[3]

In what follows, I will argue that Judith Butler is wrong about militant antifascism. I would like to begin with a statement of the method and scope of the critique. There are two lines of inquiry I will not pursue. First, I will focus on Butler's arguments concerning nonviolence, but I will not dispute how they buttress their arguments through the work of theorists such as Michel Foucault, Walter Benjamin, Sigmund Freud, Melanie Klein, or Frantz Fanon. Second, I am not concerned with situating their work within debates in nonviolence studies or peace studies. It has been received positively in several forums for leftist academics, and far from greeting their case for nonviolence with skepticism as Butler anticipates, several reviewers fault them for not defending nonviolence vigorously enough.[4] These faults notwithstanding, S. Shankar observes that, given Butler's stature, *The Force of Nonviolence* "places the problem of nonviolence — and it surely is a problem — now firmly on the contemporary agenda of critical theory, an institutionalized discursive field to whose emergence and constitution Butler has been indispensable."[5] Shankar's comment demonstrates the necessity of meeting Butler's work with a principled and militant antifascist rejoinder.

Some militants might dismiss Butler's work out of hand as a variety of postmodernism or intellectualism. Natasha Lennard, in a generally illuminating review, cautiously ascribes Butler's failures to ingrained academicism.[6] However, in my view, Butler's position is emblematic of some of the core contradictions and problems with liberal approaches to both violence and antifascism. Militants need to face these problems head on.

Philosophy has the critical task of demarcating boundaries within a given theoretical terrain.[7] If we consider social struggle as a terrain including a number of contending theoretical frameworks, then one task of a critical analysis involves mapping the relationships between certain theories and their specific provinces. Militant antifascist theory is — or ought to be — formulated within a broader revolutionary horizon. In practice, though, it has a concrete role within broader anticapitalist struggle as a form of community self-defense which combats emergent street-level far-right organizing. By contrast, liberal antifascism maintains that far-right organizing can be curtailed by the inculcation of democratic norms, a generally free exchange of ideas, and the reinforcement of existing social institutions. But liberal antifascist organizing then cedes organizational ground to these liberal social institutions, established media platforms, and — for the suppression of far-right movements, should the occasion arise — law enforcement. On this basis, I would conclude that liberal antifascism inhabits a "narrower" terrain than militant antifascism: there is a smaller field of possible praxis, and some theoretical questions — such as the relationship between law enforcement and antifascist organizing — remain unanswered or mired in contradictions.

I will outline a critique of Butler's position in order to show that their account of nonviolence and their politics of grievability occupy a narrow practical terrain. In *The Force of Nonviolence*, they take an unconventional approach to the defense of nonviolence. Most debates about nonviolence and violence focus on moral, political, or practical justifications for adopting certain tactics or strategies rather than others. One might argue, for

GENEALOGIES OF ANTIFASCISM

example, that nonviolent tactics are more effective than violent tactics. For Butler, these are "instrumentalist" approaches to the problem. They propose a "non-instrumentalist" framework that analyzes nonviolence as a form of world-building, based on the recognition and expression of interdependency, vulnerability, grievability, and radical egalitarianism — social bonds which, on their view, open political spaces to resist violence. As Butler writes, nonviolence is "a social and political practice undertaken in concert, culminating in a form of resistance to systemic forms of destruction coupled with a commitment to world building that honors global interdependency of the kind that embodies ideals of economic, social, and political freedom and equality" (21). As Butler admits, nonviolence serves as a radical imaginary or utopic horizon.

Butler observes that we cannot examine violence in isolation, for violence is always interpreted within a frame. Indeed, violence is not one distinct thing. It may refer to physical force ("the figure of the blow"), systemic violence, or speech (for example, a political figure may license violence in their public utterances). Different frames define violence differently, and these differences have political ramifications. Furthermore, they note, any discussion of violence arises within a discursive field in which the state conducts a "political war, as it were, at the level of public semantics," by framing nonviolent resistance as violence, while framing state violence as "self-defense" (3).

Despite these observations, in *The Force of Nonviolence*, Butler never explicitly situates the frame or vantage point from whence *they* speak. Therefore, I will begin by foregrounding the following critique of *The Force of Nonviolence* by comparing it to their position in "Protest, Violent and Nonviolent," a commentary on far-right protests in Berkeley, California in 2017 that reveals the practical side — and thus the narrow political horizon — of Butler's politics. Similar philosophical arguments undergird both works. But in "Protest, Violent and Nonviolent" they focus on a proposed electoral path to defeating Trump and far-right social forces. Thus, when framing the significance of the various groups involved in the demonstration (and counter-demonstration) they commit an interpretive error that is common to many analyses of social movements. As Stanislav Vysotsky observes:

> Classical analyses of social movements often focus on the way in which movements engage with state and economic actors in an attempt to influence policy changes … . Even the literature on countermovements or, more commonly, opposing movements, often looks at movements that operate on two sides of a policy domain rather than as movements developed in direct opposition to one another.[8]

Militant antifascism, however, is directly focused on countering opposing movements of far-right and fascist organizing. The three way fight approach positions militant practice against two contending social forces: the capitalist system (and its concomitant ideology) and system-oppositional far-right organizing. The immediate goal of antifascist organizing is, on this view, to apply a diversity of tactics to undermine far-right movements. Butler's political orientation is closer to the classical social movement view. As I will argue, their politics of grievability points toward a form of redress for vulnerable groups through recognition. In "Protest, Violent and Nonviolent," they interpret the antagonism between far-right demonstrators and antifascist counterprotestors as a contest to manifest a popular political consensus, and, given that the far-right was greatly outnumbered, "that would have been enough to 'demonstrate' that the consensus was clearly against them."[9] But violence, Butler argues, undermines the communication and inculcation of democratic norms, which in turn deepens the crisis of democracy signaled by Donald Trump's electoral victory in 2016. They write:

> Violence only compounds the sense of hopelessness and skepticism about the possibility of practicing

democracy, when that is precisely what we need most: the exercise of judgment, freedom, and power within the sphere of politics that can activate the true majority to drive Trump and his crew out of office .... Protest is a way of voting on and with the streets, asserting a sense of the people that remains radically unrepresented by the "representative" government that exists. An assembly outside of the established assemblies, protest establishes the space and time for those disenfranchised to show up and be counted even when, or precisely when, the electoral count has failed them.[10]

Butler outlines how nonviolent, liberal protestors might attempt to demonstrate popular consensus against the Trump administration. I categorize their politics as a form of liberal antifascism because they appeal to the inculcation of democratic norms ("the exercise of judgment, freedom, and power within the sphere of politics") as the counterweight to far-right organizing. Furthermore, when we assess the argument of *The Force of Non-violence* below, I believe it is illustrative of their politics that they describe protest as "a way of voting on and with the streets ... [which] establishes the space and time for those disenfranchised to show up and be counted even when, or precisely when, the electoral count has failed them."

We will ask, as Butler once did in a different context, "what relations of domination and exclusion are inadvertently sustained when representation becomes the sole focus of politics?"[11] By focusing on a politics of representation and recognition, their account is only a partial view of the conflict between militant antifascism and the far right. They contend that the far-right demonstrators were defeated by the superior numbers of antifascist counterprotestors. However, superior numbers are not sufficient to undermine far-right organizing. Fascists are well aware of the stigma attached to their ideology and activities; indeed, this stigma helps explain why doxxing is an effective antifascist tactic.[12] While far-right groups do attempt to normalize their ideology within many social spheres, their street-level organizing in 2017 was oriented around bringing online communities into public spaces in order to both recruit new members and to harass and intimidate their political opponents. Thus, one of the core militant strategic questions was (and still is): what tactics most effectively undermine far-right organizing? Superior numbers may help—and they seemed to help in the aftermath of the Unite the Right rally in Charlottesville, Virginia, in August 2017. However, a superior number of counterprotestors is neither necessary nor sufficient for undermining far-right organizing. Militant antifascists aim to undermine recruitment efforts and provide emancipatory community self-defense, and their strategic or tactical choices must be judged on the effectiveness of those efforts. Butler, however, applies the rationale of liberal antifascist strategies to militant antifascism, and hence they only provide a partial view of the political terrain and what is at stake in the confrontation between fascists and antifascists in militant struggle.

OUTLINE OF THE CRITICAL ARGUMENT

I have foregrounded the following critique of Butler's defense of nonviolence by outlining the liberal antifascist parameters of their politics because I seek to show that their theory of political resistance is applicable to a narrow field of political practice. Despite being written as the far right emerged as a significant and dangerous political force in the United States, *The Force of Nonviolence* focuses almost exclusively on nonviolent resistance to state violence. Such an analysis cannot account for a three way fight.

Nonetheless, Butler is an important public philosopher whose work warrants an in-depth critical analysis—for their arguments express the contradictions and anxieties of liberal antifascism and nonviolent resistance. In *The Force of Nonviolence*, they make several interrelated arguments about violence and nonviolence, and I seek to disentangle the argumentative threads and address the core claims against the militant antifascist "diversity of tactics," which I categorize as a form of emancipatory community self-defense. Hence I have divided the critique into five sections.

In section two, I will focus on Butler's critique of the "self" of self-defense. I will contend that they fail to distinguish between common-sense notions of self-defense and a concept of emancipatory community self-defense. In sum, the critique of common-sense notions of self-defense is not sufficient to refute a militant and emancipatory justification for self-defense.

In sections three and four, I will reconstruct Butler's politics through an analysis of their concepts of interdependency, vulnerability, and grievability. I will then undertake a comparative reading of *The Force of Nonviolence* and three works by Simone de Beauvoir: *The Ethics of Ambiguity* (1947), "An Eye For An Eye" (1946), and *The Force of Circumstance* (1963). I will argue that Beauvoir also makes a strong case to treat interdependency and grief as political categories, although, against Butler, she concludes that doing so could warrant the use of emancipatory violence rather than nonviolence.

After demonstrating that neither the critique of the "self" of self-defense nor the concern for interdependency and grievability necessitate nonviolence, in sections five and six I address what I consider to be Butler's foundational objection to violence: the problem of license. They contend that the use of violence licenses others to use violence legitimately, and thus violence spirals into a self-propelling cycle untethered from the intentions of those who wield it. When we reflect upon the last six years of militant antifascist opposition to far-right organizing, it is notable that this supposedly ineluctable cycle of violence did not happen. Thus, in section five, I will argue that the problem of license ignores how contending social movements actually discursively justify violence. I will then conclude by returning to the concept of emancipatory community self-defense in section six, in order to show that the concept does not license far-right violence, and, finally, to define what makes community self-defense *emancipatory*.

2. BUTLER'S INSUFFICIENT CRITICISM OF SELF-DEFENSE

Given that militant antifascists justify their tactics as a part of community self-defense, Butler's critique of self-defense constitutes their most direct, albeit implicit, critique of militant antifascism. They contend that the "self" of self-defense is embedded in the political and social hierarchies within which it arises, and thus not all selves are extended the right to self-defense (12). It is not controversial to question the "self" presupposed by common-sense notions of self-defense. Numerous critics do so. In *Loaded: A Disarming History of the Second Amendment*, Roxanne Dunbar-Ortiz traces the social and political history of the right to bear arms, showing that during the early period of the North American colonial project "settler-militias and armed households were institutionalized for the destruction and control of Native peoples, communities, and nations. With the expansion of plantation agriculture, by the late 1600s they were also used as 'slave patrols,' forming the basis of U.S. police culture after enslaving people was illegalized."[13] This history shaped the discussion and emergence of the right to bear arms and the common-sense notion of self-defense, and this notion is also shaped by a contemporary U.S. gun culture that, Dunbar-Ortiz observes, "has entitled white nationalism, racialized dominance, and social control through violence."[14] The right to self-defense is formally recognized under the law, but the norms that guide its practical recognition are embedded in the racial and gender hierarchies present in society. Butler points, for instance, to the different verdicts reached in the trials of George Zimmerman and Marissa Alexander, whose respective cases were both prosecuted in the same Florida county. Zimmerman was acquitted for the murder of Trayvon Martin, while Marissa Alexander was sentenced to twenty years in prison for attempting to defend herself from sexual assault (117). Within a settler-colonial Canadian context, Gina Starblanket and Dallas Hunt provide an in-depth examination of the narratives surrounding the recent (2018) trial of Gerald Stanley, a white settler who was charged with—and ultimately acquitted of—the second degree murder of Colten Boushie, a twenty-two-year-old member of the Cree Red Pheasant First Nation. They observe that Stanley's defense "relied upon racialized associations between Indigeneity and deviance, troublemaking, and terror, and corresponding narratives of settler independence, industry, and lawfulness—without ever having to speak about race. It is precisely because these narratives are so deeply normalized in the prairies that they were able to make sense to the jury and, ultimately, help configure the outcome of the case."[15]

Yet the question remains: is Butler's critique relevant to the concept of self-defense upheld by militant antifascism? It is not, because they fail to differentiate between common-sense notions of self-defense, to which their criticisms are applicable, and emancipatory community self-defense, to which they are not. I define the two categories of self-defense as follows:

> *The common-sense notion of self-defense* conceives of self-defense as an exceptional moment within a political continuum that runs from individual right to state violence. According to this notion, the individual assumes that they are protected by law enforcement; but, when there is an "imminent threat" and law enforcement is not present, an individual has the natural or self-evident right to protect their person, property, and family.

> *Emancipatory community self-defense* fosters autonomy and solidarity for socially vulnerable groups; it is organized against the antagonism of police oppression, so there is no presumed continuum between community action and police power; and this communal form of self-defense is often not protected by the "right" of self-defense extended by the state.

In my view, Butler's critique applies exclusively to common-sense notions of self-defense, which situate an individual's right to self-defense as an exceptional moment (an imminent threat) that occurs in the absence of law enforcement. Self-defense, according to common-sense notions, is generally considered a private, individual act rather than a political act. In this case, an act of self-defense does not challenge the social and political parameters of an oppressive society; instead, its meaning arises within those parameters. Unsurprisingly, when the theme of "self-defense" (the scare quotes here are deliberate) is politicized—consider the right-wing-celebrity status enjoyed momentarily by Mark and Patricia McCloskey in 2020—it is celebrated as a defense of (oppressive) society.

Butler contends that the received notion of self-defense belies a "closet communitarianism" whereby the individual protects those who are "proximate and similar" to themselves (11, 53). In these cases, the "self" of self-defense "can function as a kind of regime, including as part of its extended self all those who bear similitude to one's color, class, and privilege, thus expelling from the regime of the subject/self all those marked by difference within that economy" (12). In other words, in an oppressive society, only some selves receive the entitlement to self-defense, while others are excluded on the basis of their marginalized social position. Butler rightly criticizes communitarian appeals to self-defense by those in power, who use these appeals to justify and fortify structures of exclusion and oppression. They also rightly criticize advocates of nonviolence who permit individual exceptions for self-defense, because these exceptions are grounded in—not critical of—assumptions implicit in the general political parameters of common-sense notions, though as we will see Butler also falls into this trap.

Now we must resolve a critical question about the applicability of Butler's critique of self-defense. As I have noted, they do not differentiate between common-sense notions of self-defense and emancipatory community self-defense. It seems that Butler believes that their criticisms hold regardless of what type of self-defense is involved. Thus, their criticisms would apply to emancipatory approaches to self-defense such as militant antifascism or the armed Black freedom struggle. Is it adequate to reject these organizational forms as communitarian or exclusionary? In "Protest, Violent and Nonviolent," they criticize certain black bloc actions on these grounds. As I will argue in section six, their assertions about contemporary militants on this point are questionable. As a further example, the history of the armed Black civil rights struggle shows that it is incorrect to assume that sociologically homogenous oppressed groups necessarily practice self-defense on communitarian grounds: activists such as Robert F. Williams or the Deacons for Defense were willing to risk their lives to protect white and often Northern and middle-class civil rights activists in the South. Even were this not the case, we cannot necessarily conclude that an oppressed but sociologically homogenous group's use of self-defense is illegitimate because of the supposedly homogeneous makeup of the community.

Yet Butler's citations make it evident that they are aware of countervailing interpretations of emancipatory concepts of community self-defense. They credit Elsa Dorlin, author of *Self-Defense: A Philosophy of Violence*, for the observation that "only some selves are regarded as entitled to self-defense" (12). However, Dorlin contends that "the history of self-defense is polarized, marked by continuous opposition of *two* antagonistic expressions of the defense of the 'self'" (my emphasis), an opposition between a juridical-political notion of self-defense and a "martial ethics of the self" practiced by embattled communities.[16] Butler also cites *Setting Sights: Histories and Reflections on Community Armed Self-Defense*, an anthology which contains numerous essays—written by veterans and participants in a wide variety of social movements—that criticize communitarian grounds for action and anticipate their critique of the "self" and self-defense. Chad Kautzer's contribution in particular foregrounds a critical concept of self-defense through the criticism of the concept of the sovereign subject of self-defense and the recognition of group-differentiated social vulnerability. In other words, advocates of emancipatory community self-defense have already carried out the kind of critique Butler believes would be necessary to permit its justification.

In addition, the essays collected in *Setting Sights* critically engage with advocates of community self-defense who justify it on the basis of common-sense notions. We can find appeals to the constitutional right to self-defense by Malcolm X or the Black Panther Party for Self-Defense (BPP), but their respective organizational strategies reflect features of emancipatory community self-defense, insofar as they aimed to build community autonomy and solidarity against the countervailing force of the open antagonism of police oppression and white supremacy. There is a telling passage in *Negroes with Guns* (1962), in which Robert F. Williams challenges not the *state's* presumed monopoly on violence, but "the exclusive monopoly of violence practiced by white racists."[17] In a similar vein, Kautzer argues that appeals by Malcolm X or the BPP to constitutional rights or common-sense notions of self-defense were attempts to "normalize black people defending themselves against the violence of white rule."[18] However, Black freedom struggles didn't appeal to common-sense notions of self-defense to merely justify protections for individuals in the absence of law enforcement, they did so to present plain-language justifications for emancipatory community self-defense and a much broader revolutionary social struggle for liberation.[19]

In sum, as I have shown, Butler's critique of self-defense raises more questions than it answers. By failing to distinguish between different types of self-defense, they seem to maintain that their criticisms of common-sense notions of self-defense apply to other practices of self-defense. They raise concerns about how George Zimmerman walked for the murder of Trayvon Martin while Marissa Alexander received a twenty-year sentence for attempting to defend herself, but they do not provide the grounds to justify self-defense in cases like Alexander's. They do not discuss the histories of community self-defense, but when we reconstruct and flesh out the ramifications of Butler's position vis-à-vis armed civil rights struggle, their broad appeals to global solidarity are, as Fanon once said of certain First World intellectuals, "hedged about with all sorts of fundamental restrictions as to [those movements'] objectives."[20]

Here, I have focused on Butler's critique of self-defense in the Introduction to *The Force of Nonviolence*. Later in the book Butler indicates in passing that their position admits of exceptional cases of self-defense (56). Though they criticize the un-examined "self" who is entitled to the use of self-defense, who is presumed in the social imaginary to be white and male sovereign subject, they do not explore how the exceptional character of self-defense is embedded in common-sense notions as well. As I have noted, according to these notions, the act of self-defense is an exceptional moment that occurs in the absence of law enforcement. If my characterization is correct, then Butler uncritically accepts one important aspect of the common-sense notion: the continuum of protection by law enforcement. While they present their work as a critique of state power and violence, Butler ultimately leaves the oppressed, who organize in the midst of open hostility and opposition from law enforcement, without grounds for community self-defense.

3. BUTLER'S POLITICS OF GRIEVABILITY

BUTLER'S LIBERAL HORIZONS

I have shown that Butler's critique of the "self" of self-defense does not apply to forms of emancipatory community self-defense, and hence it does not apply to militant antifascism. Indeed, their treatment of self-defense risks rebounding against embattled groups who organize community action in the face of law enforcement hostility and antagonism.

In this section, I will examine Butler's argument that a practical and philosophical concern for social relationships characterized by interdependency, vulnerability, and grievability necessitates nonviolence. I will argue that their politics of grievability entails a narrowly applicable practice grounded primarily in the demand for state recognition that all lives ought to be grievable. Butler contends that domination and oppression are grounded on a distinction, made by the state or the "dominant frame" of discourse, between lives that are grievable (that is, lives that would be counted as a loss) and those that are ungrievable. Their politics of grievability asserts that all lives are grievable, and hence they demand the reorganization of social and political institutions to reduce or eliminate social vulnerability. In other words, this politics, though Butler hesitates to frame it in these terms, seeks to influence and transform governmental policy and the "dominant frame" of the public sphere. In their view, political resistance involves asserting the universal and egalitarian right of grievability against state violence. Butler argues that this recognition of grievability constitutes a "utopic horizon" for politics, but I will contend that the politics of grievability as they present it falls squarely within liberal parameters of political participation. Indeed, if we set aside Butler's conceptual terminology, we discern a fairly standard justification for nonviolent resistance: activists engage in nonviolent civil disobedience as part of a demand for a universal political right, and when state power or an organized opposition engage in violence it reveals how violence is used to protect the interests of a particular class or group. It is a narrowly applicable practice, appealing to the political conscience of a ruling hegemonic bloc.

Here, we encounter a fork in the road of interpretation. We might choose to dismiss the concepts of interdependency, vulnerability, and grievability as irretrievably trapped in a poststructuralist iteration of liberal political theory. I would warn against this path, which would expel these concepts from revolutionary theory and occlude part of the terrain of struggle. As Butler recalls, they began considering the political character of grievability during the AIDS crisis in the 1980s.[21] Furthermore, the concept of social vulnerability plays an important role in abolitionist literature and some critical theories of community self-defense, for example, in the work of Ruth Wilson Gilmore

GENEALOGIES OF ANTIFASCISM

or Chad Kautzer. And we will engage with works by Beauvoir that factor similar concepts into her understanding of antifascist struggle.

After outlining Butler's politics of grievability, I will argue that a concern for social relationships characterized by inter-dependency, vulnerability, and grievability does not necessitate nonviolence. I will show, through an analysis oriented by Simone de Beauvoir's *Ethics of Ambiguity*, that a concern for these social relationships may, in certain situations, permit violent political action. Through this reading of Beauvoir, I will demonstrate that the respect and recognition of interdependency, vulnerability, or grievability may justify the use of violence to protect these social relationships.

Beauvoir may seem like an unlikely point of comparison. Yet Butler has engaged with existentialist figures throughout their career. As is often recognized, *Gender Trouble* (1990) includes a critique of Beauvoir's *Second Sex*. They have also written commentaries on Beauvoir's "Must We Burn Sade?" and Sartre's preface to Fanon's *Wretched of the Earth*.[22] And while they return in various texts—including *The Force of Nonviolence*—to Fanon's treatment of violence, they have not to my knowledge addressed Beauvoir's defense of antifascist and emancipatory violence.

Beauvoir may also seem to be an unlikely point of comparison because she has been criticized for inadequately dispensing with Sartre's seemingly individualistic and gendered (masculine) concept of freedom.[23] Handling the broader question of gender and freedom in their respective works is beyond the scope of this essay. However, the narrower problem of freedom and individualism is within the scope. I will argue that Beauvoir situates her concept of moral and political freedom within social relationships of interdependency that carry ethical obligations toward others. I will show how, despite some similarities between their analyses, Beauvoir draws starkly different conclusions than Butler about the legitimacy of emancipatory violence. Furthermore, I will contend that a reconstruction of a theory of interdependency in Beauvoir's work demonstrates that already in *The Ethics of Ambiguity*, she is concerned with reconciling existentialism and historical materialism. As Sonia Kruks observes, the "vital place of Marxist materialism" in Beauvoir's work "remains woefully under-explored," due in part to the hostility of later anglophone interpreters to Marxism.[24] As I will argue, Beauvoir anchors her theory of interdependency in class struggle. Indeed, her approach anticipates Sartre's later view that existentialism's philosophical purpose is to conceptualize the "margin of real freedom" that emerges within situations of oppression and domination.

BUTLER'S POLITICS OF GRIEVABILITY

Butler frames what I will call their "politics of grievability" as a practice of world-building that acknowledges the conditions of interdependency, vulnerability, and grievability. They present their position as an alternative to the individualism of social contract theory and neoliberalism. The foundational premise of social contract theory posits "man" as a self-sufficient adult; that humans are born and live as children in a condition of dependency on others is disavowed. By contrast, Butler contends that all social life is grounded in interdependency: as much as one may develop a sense of individuality and self-sufficiency, at no point does an individual "escape" the fundamental conditions of interdependency — their world continues to be facilitated by kinship structures, social structures, and the environment.

For Butler, interdependency forms the basis of both vulnerability and obligations to the other. Vulnerability is not an individual predicament, but rather a non-eliminable possibility of interdependency:

> Vulnerability is not exactly the same as dependency. I depend on someone, something, or some condition in order to live. But when that person disappears, or that object is withdrawn, or that social institution falls apart, I am vulnerable to being dispossessed, abandoned, or exposed in ways that may well prove unlivable. (46)

Butler's account entails two categories of vulnerability. The first is referred to as "corporeal vulnerability" in Butler's book *Precarious Life* (2004).[25] Corporeal vulnerability means that as human beings "we are, as bodies, outside ourselves and for another."[26] In addition, I think it must entail that human beings are vulnerable to the lack of basic needs: food, water, medical care, or other necessities which, when absent, would make life unlivable. Along with corporeal vulnerability, there is social vulnerability: vulnerability that exposes some groups to increased risk of precariousness, injury, or death; Butler refers to this increased risk as the "unequal distribution of vulnerability" (71). Racism is an example of social vulnerability. Butler cites Ruth Wilson Gilmore: "racism, specifically, is the state-sanctioned or extralegal production and exploitation of group-differentiated vulnerability to premature death" (109).[27]

It is worth noting, before moving on, that one major problem with Butler's work involves the ambiguity of vulnerability. They consistently argue that the politics of grievability involves the recognition of vulnerability. But which type? Butler's position, in my view, remains ambivalent. It seems that their politics aims to ameliorate some socially unequal exposure to *individuals'* corporeal vulnerability within existing social institutions rather than extirpating systemic structures of *collective* social vulnerability.[28] Indeed, the limits of Butler's politics may be discerned when we consider the problem of social vulnerability in relation to law enforcement. In my view, based on their defense of nonviolence, they accept the liberal antifascist norm that law enforcement will curtail far-right organizing when it presents a credible threat. As a consequence, their position necessitates that embattled communities, who might otherwise engage in emancipatory community self-defense, risk further social vulnerability by eliciting law enforcement protections instead. We will return to this problem below.

Butler contends that individuals become socially vulnerable when they are not seen to be grievable. In Butler's view, the concept of grievability is necessary to interpret violence: "life has to be grievable—that is, its loss has to be conceptualizable *as a loss*—for an interdiction against violence and destruction to include that life among those living beings to be safeguarded from violence" (58). Grievability has three characteristics. First, to be grievable is a category applied to the living; as such, those who are grievable must be safeguarded from violence. Second, those who are grievable are interpellated as such: they know the loss of their lives would count as a loss (59). And third, grievability has a claim to the future. The loss of a such a life is grieved both for the present loss and for "the conjectured future of a life as an indefinite potential" (75–76). Conversely, we may also define what is an ungrievable life. An ungrievable life is not counted as a loss. In addition, an ungrievable life is exposed to violence and premature death, such as Gilmore defines racism, "the state-sanctioned or extralegal production and exploitation of group-differentiated vulnerability to premature death." And, third, we may conclude that those who are ungrievable are denied the recognition that the loss of their life is a loss; they are refused an interpellation that their lives would count as a loss.

For Butler, grievability is the crux of both oppression and an egalitarian politics and ethics: "Grievability governs the way in which living creatures are managed, and it proves to be an integral dimension of biopolitics and of ways of thinking about equality among the living" (56). In Foucault's terms, biopower divides a population between those who it "makes live" and those who it "lets die." Like Foucault, Butler argues that state power or government has shifted from sovereign power to biopolitics (though it may be that for Butler both sovereign power and biopower are two distinct but overlapping techniques of government). Both focus on the biopolitical function of state power, which involves managing populations according to grievability. Butler contrasts the politics of grievability with the biopolitics of contemporary power. They frame the politics of grievability as egalitarian because it asserts, against the imposition of social inequality between those who are grievable and those who are not, that all lives are grievable.

For Butler, protests are one paradigmatic form of nonviolent resistance. Protest challenges what Butler refers to as a "dominant frame." In order to define a "dominant frame," we may turn to their book *Precarious Life*, where they observe that "the prohibition on certain forms of public grieving itself constitutes the public sphere on the basis of such a prohibition."[29] Protest resists the exclusion of a publicly ungrievable group through the public performance of grief. Protest *forces* the grievability of the ungrievable—it emerges as a form of recognition that challenges public disavowal.

In interviews. Butler points to Black Lives Matter as a form of militant mourning that challenges the political coordinates of the dominant discourse.[30] Thus, from Butler's perspective, Black Lives Matter protests, as public grieving, seek to "establish new terms of acknowledgement and resistance. This would be a form of militant grieving that breaks into the public sphere of appearance, inaugurating a new constellation of space and time" (106). In both cases—with symbolic recognition or with protests—Butler presents the politics of grievability as a counter-institutional political force, a form of political struggle that opposes the biopolitical apparatuses that refuse to recognize that all lives are grievable. They frame the politics of grievability as egalitarian because it asserts, against the imposition of social inequality between those who are grievable and those who are not, that all lives are grievable. Universal grievability, for Butler, functions as a utopic horizon for reorganizing social relationships around the recognition of interdependency and shared vulnerability. As Alexander Livingston summarizes: "once the self is seen in relational terms, sustained through bonds that exceed sovereign control, the goal of defending the self is turned inside out, since it must now encompass protecting and expanding the social infrastructure through which lives can be more equitably lived. Acts of violence that put these bonds at risk are not simply immoral, they are self-defeating."[31] I will argue, by contrast, that Butler only shows how violence is self-defeating within the specific political parameters of the politics of grievability.

4. BEAUVOIR AS A CRITIC OF BUTLER

Though Butler never cites *The Ethics of Ambiguity*, there are passages of *The Force of Nonviolence* that evoke Beauvoir's important, albeit often neglected, essay. Beauvoir observes that interdependency makes both moral freedom and oppression possible, while Butler writes: "the obligations that bind us to one another follow from the condition of interdependency that makes our lives possible but that can also be one condition for exploitation and violence" (46). Both maintain that an "open future" is an important condition for practical freedom; as Butler phrases it, "we might say, without that open future, a life is merely existing, but it is not living" (100–101).

Nonetheless, I do not want to overstate the similarities. Butler acknowledges that interdependency can be a condition for exploitation and violence but does not analyze the specific mechanisms of systemic violence aside from the biopolitical separation between grievable and ungrievable lives, while Beauvoir explores interdependency in relation to the social division of labor, as exploitative work, under capitalism and colonialism. (In this light, we may then consider parts of the *The Second Sex* as an examination of the exploitative and oppressive character of the gendered division of labor.) In addition, I am interested in how they arrive at very different conclusions regarding the legitimacy of emancipatory violence. For Butler, that phrase would be a contradiction in terms, while Beauvoir concludes that the oppressed have the moral justification to use violent means in the fight for liberation. I will argue that Beauvoir shows how interdependency or grief, far from necessitating nonviolence, may justify emancipatory violence.

BEAUVOIR ON INTERDEPENDENCY AND OPPRESSION

The Ethics of Ambiguity is often treated as a commentary on Sartre's philosophy because Beauvoir often casts her discussion as a defense of his work. Nonetheless, she advances distinct solutions to criticisms raised against existentialism. In Chapter 1, she responds to criticisms of Sartre's concept of freedom by distinguishing between ontological freedom and moral freedom.[32] In *Being and Nothingness* (1943) and other works from the period, Sartre tends to disregard how circumstances could constrain the choices a person might make. Years later, he explains his position as a response to the circumstances of World War II:

> there was a very simple problem during the Resistance — ultimately, only a question of courage. One had to accept the risks involved in what one was doing, that is, of being imprisoned or deported. But beyond this? A Frenchman was either for the Germans or against them, there was no other option … . The result was that I concluded that in any circumstances, there is always a possible choice.[33]

Sartre's later summary is an accurate description of his position from the mid-1940s. He grants that external circumstances might narrow an individual's possible choices, but he does not see that as constraint. Instead, he maintains that one chooses *despite* circumstances and not *due to* them. On his view, treating external circumstances as mitigating factors in one's choices disavows one's responsibility for them (i.e., bad faith). By discounting the conditions that factor into choices, though, Sartre seems to suggest that all choices are equivalent as long as they are free. However, not all free choices are equivalent: all conditions being equal, I doubt he would accept that holding a private opinion against the Occupation is meaningfully equivalent to armed resistance against it.

After the war, both Sartre and Beauvoir sought to align existentialism with the political and philosophical commitments of historical materialism. Though Beauvoir later criticizes her attempts to align the two during this period, the distinction she draws between ontological freedom and moral freedom as well as her concept of interdependency both mark advances beyond Sartre's work.[34]

Beauvoir introduces the distinction between ontological and moral freedom in order to overcome the following objection: "Does not the presence of a so to speak natural freedom contradict the notion of moral freedom? What meaning can there be in the words *to will oneself free*, since at the beginning we *are* free?"[35] Later, in *The Ethics of Ambiguity*, she returns to a more pointed example of this objection, which asserts that I can will nothing for others, since others *are* free.[36] The first objection involves a conceptual paradox between being and acting: if I *am* free, then how do any of my actions make me more free? This problem is mere philosophical play compared to the gravity of the second objection, which asserts that I have no obligations toward others because they are already free, and thus any injustice they face in a situation is the product of their own choices. In both cases, Beauvoir contends that these objections have confused two levels of analysis. She defines ontological freedom as the original spontaneity of human existence: "every man is originally free, in the sense that he spontaneously casts himself into the world."[37] Human existence is free in the same way that one observes (as Beauvoir does at the beginning of the book) that human beings are finite; i.e., mortal and limited by the actions of others. In other words, ontological freedom is descriptive: humans are free because they exist with no a priori existential purpose.

For Beauvoir, moral freedom is the commitment one makes to projects, such as enriching oneself through the extraction of surplus-value or joining a revolutionary movement. The success of these endeavors relies on material means and interactions with others. But, fundamentally, it involves commitment to certain values and the rejection of others. To summarize, she discusses ontological freedom as a description of human existence, whereas her outline of the actual ethics of ambiguity involves analyzing moral freedom: how choices commit us to concrete values and projects which within our social world are sometimes incompatible, in contradiction, or irreconcilable. It is because human projects conflict—including conflicts such as the

antagonism between the proletariat and the bourgeoisie—that
Beauvoir deems it necessary to analyze the relationship between
freedom and violence.

For Beauvoir, both freedom and oppression are possibilities which arise on the basis of interdependency. Indeed, she
observes that interdependency

> explains why oppression is possible and why it is odi-
> ous. As we have seen, my freedom, in order to fulfill
> itself, requires that it emerge into an open future: it is
> other men who open the future to me, it is they who,
> setting up the world of tomorrow, define my future;
> but if, instead of allowing me to participate in this
> constructive movement, they oblige me to consume my
> transcendence in vain ... then they are cutting me off
> from the future, they are changing me into a thing.[38]

Beauvoir scholarship recognizes the importance of her reference to interdependency because it epitomizes how her concept
of freedom differs from Sartre's. Sartre, at least in *Being and
Nothingness*, characterizes intersubjectivity as necessarily conflictual, meaning that he struggles to account for solidarity.[39] For
Beauvoir, intersubjectivity is instead ambiguous—it opens the
possibility for both solidarity and oppression. To my knowledge,
though, Beauvoir scholars have not presented a robust analysis
of the relationship between interdependency and oppression in
The Ethics of Ambiguity.

According to Beauvoir, oppression divides the world into
two groups:

> those who edify humanity by thrusting it ahead of itself
> and those who are condemned to mark time hopelessly
> in order to merely support the collectivity; their life is
> a pure repetition of mechanical gestures; their leisure
> is just about sufficient for them to regain their strength;
> the oppressor feeds himself on their transcendence

and refuses to extend it [their transcendence] by a free recognition.[40]

In other words, at the most basic level, oppression produces an antagonism between at least two groups. In *The Ethics of Ambiguity*, Beauvoir often uses class and colonialism as examples of oppression because they present clear lines of conflict between the bourgeoisie and the proletariat or the colonizer and the colonized. But exploitation and oppression are complex social phenomena. Hence Beauvoir isolates three interlocking facets of oppression: dehumanization, the suppression of transcendence, and the expropriation of material means.

First, a situation of oppression dehumanizes the oppressed by treating them as things or objects. There are two ways to treat a human as a thing. In the first sense, the oppressor could treat the oppressed as merely a means to their ends. In this sense, the oppressed are treated as mere instruments of the oppressor.[41] In the second sense, dehumanization is a form of existential violence that exposes the oppressed to one or more of the following: the denial of one's political autonomy, the violation of bodily autonomy, or the social vulnerability to premature death. In sum, exploitation, injury, or violence to the oppressed is not counted as an injustice or a loss.[42]

Second, oppression suppresses the transcendence of the oppressed. As an existential or ontological concept, transcendence is part of the temporality of human freedom; that is, human freedom transcends the present situation toward the future through projects. As a moral or political concept, a project is the end to which a human being's actions aim. Exploitation, to follow Beauvoir's claim here, circumscribes the horizon of the future of the oppressed by limiting the moral or political transcendence of their projects to immanent tasks or needs. Furthermore, oppression might involve the permanent suppression of transcendence through injury or death.

Finally, oppression involves the expropriation of the material production or material means of the oppressed; or, as

Beauvoir states, the oppressor "feeds" on the transcendence of the oppressed. In my view, she means that the oppressor suppresses the future possibilities in concretely material ways; for example, by the expropriation of surplus-value or the dispossession of land. The processes of expropriation or dispossession also entail the reproduction of these structures of oppression, which expropriate the material means to enable one to realize one's projects concretely.

At this point we are prepared to interpret how Beauvoir's theory of oppression illuminates her concept of interdependency. Although Butler mentions that interdependency can be a condition for both obligations and oppression, they do not explain how. Instead, they focus primarily on how the recognition of interdependency entails social obligations. Beauvoir, by contrast, demonstrates how we are interdependent when it comes to meeting our immanent social necessities and in enabling and realizing our freedom through projects. And, for Beauvoir, systems of exploitation are able to reproduce themselves because they are able to exploit the necessity of our immanent social needs. The question is: how?

Beauvoir divides the practical field of human activity into two realms: a realm of immanence and a realm of transcendence (of course, this is a conceptual distinction more than a concrete, lived distinction). The oppressor feeds off the transcendence of the oppressed, or, in other words, the oppressed is relegated to the domain of immanence. In *The Ethics of Ambiguity*, as with *The Second Sex*, immanence signifies a domain of repetition and necessity. In the former, Beauvoir repeatedly characterizes oppressed groups as "trapped" in immanence and cut off from transcendence.[43] In the latter, she demonstrates that a woman's situation is largely frustrated by her relegation to the domain of immanence (e.g., the private life of the household) where "she is absorbed in producing or maintaining things that are never more than means—food, clothes, lodging."[44] Human existence cannot escape immanence, which involves meeting basic needs or necessities. However, a situation of oppression utilizes a social division of labor which relegates an oppressed group to the production and reproduction of social necessities. Hence, as Beauvoir writes, the oppressed "support the collectivity; their life is a pure repetition of mechanical gestures."[45]

Yet the freedom of the oppressed is not entirely foreclosed by oppression. Beauvoir recognizes that there is a margin of freedom for members of the oppressed, or else her existentialist politics would lapse into a mechanistic philosophy of social change that she associates with dogmatic forms of Marxism, whereby "subjectivity is re-absorbed into the objectivity of the given world; [hence] revolt, need, hope, rejection, and desire are only the resultants of external forces."[46] The domain of transcendence is opened by a margin of freedom which arises on the basis of fulfilling social needs and necessities — moral and political freedom cannot be realized without material means, collective action with others, and the horizon of an open future. Therefore, for Beauvoir, liberation does not involve an escape from interdependency or immanence but rather the emancipation of the oppressed from the domain of immanence and the elimination of toil, as well as the expansion of the possibilities of transcendence and freedom.

Interestingly enough, Beauvoir's social theory, as I have reconstructed it, anticipates the revolutionary horizon of liberation in a manner similar to Sartre's *Search for a Method* (1957), where he writes:

> We are all acquainted with the passage in which Marx alludes to that far-off time: "The realm of freedom really begins only where labour determined by necessity and external expediency ends; it lies by its very nature beyond the sphere of material production proper." As soon as there will exist *for everyone* a margin of *real* freedom beyond the production of life, Marxism will have lived out its span; a philosophy of freedom will take its place.[47]

As Marx concludes in the passage cited by Sartre: "The true realm of freedom, the development of human powers as an end in itself, begins beyond it [the realm of necessity]; though it can only flourish with this realm of necessity as its basis."[48]

Admittedly, Beauvoir does not engage with Marxism as extensively as Sartre does in *Search for a Method*. Her references to Marx, Lenin, or Trotsky are often made in passing, and her ideological relationship — beyond a critique of "Stalinism" — to different currents of Marxism is unclear. For example, she criticizes "dialectical materialism," but it is more likely that she is criticizing the dogmatism of the French Communist Party rather than "dialectical materialism" per se.[49] In any case, Beauvoir's social theory demonstrates a continuity and convergence with Sartre's attempts to square existentialism with Marxism.

BEAUVOIR'S GRIEF AND THE LIMITS
OF THE POLITICS OF GRIEVABILITY

It would be anachronistic to attribute a concept of grievability to Beauvoir. Nonetheless, she expresses a profound sense of grief in the wake of the World War II, and her reflections reveal the practical limitations of Butler's politics of grievability. In my view, Butler's politics is delimited by liberal horizons; though they hesitate to refer to rights, their demand that all lives ought to be grievable is only valid as a claim to a right. By contrast, Beauvoir explores grief within an antagonistic space of incompatible and conflicting political values. Her discussions of the trial of Robert Brasillach — a French far rightist, antisemite, collaborator, and editor-in-chief of the fascist paper *Je Suis Partout* — challenge the idea that grief or grievability can be translated into a universal "right" to the recognition of vulnerability. She shows that who (and what) we grieve is already caught up in our political and ethical commitments. For Beauvoir, it is impossible to grieve both the victims of fascism and the fascists themselves. Or, to put the problem in sharper relief, she maintains that to treat fascists as *grievable* is an insult and injustice to their victims and opponents. Indeed, I doubt Butler would disagree, but their politics of grievability couldn't justify their position.

We will examine two of Beauvoir's writings on Brasillach. The first, "An Eye for an Eye" (1946), justifies her refusal to sign a petition for clemency for Brasillach. The second, *Force of Circumstance* (1963), includes her recollections on the trial and critical reflections on her earlier writings. In "An Eye for an Eye," Beauvoir defends vengeance because it meets a fundamental human need to punish acts of "genuine evil," which involve the dehumanization of, and existential violence against, specific individuals or communities. In such cases, vengeance serves to recognize injustice through reestablishing the reciprocity between victim and perpetrator (or, more broadly, oppressed and oppressor) in order to negate this dehumanization. "The privileged case," she argues, "is one where the victim takes revenge on his own account," when, for example, concentration camp inmates attacked their jailers.[50] Furthermore, she writes,

> We were pleased with the death of Mussolini, at the hanging of Nazi executioners at Kharkov ... in so doing we have participated in their condemnation. Their crimes have struck at our own hearts. It is our values, our reasons to live that are affirmed by their punishment.[51]

The trial of Brasillach is a very different case. He was the editor-in-chief of a collaborationist paper and he never directly killed anyone, and thus it might appear that the death penalty is disproportionate to the crime. In "An Eye for an Eye," Beauvoir contends that the trial itself misrepresents the significance of punishment. The trial may have arrived at the correct verdict, but not as an affirmation of "our values, our reasons to live." The legal system renders its judgments on the basis of a supposed application of objective right. By contrast, punishment "is justified only if it is one of the moments of a wholly real conflict," and hence Beauvoir evokes throughout the essay antifascist resistance against fascists and their collaborators.[52] The collective subject of "our" values or reasons to live is the antifascist resistance. In *Force of Circumstance*, Beauvoir returns to the problem in much sharper, more personal terms:

> under his editorship, the staff of *Je Suis Partout* denounced people, specified victims, and urged the Vichy Government to enforce the wearing of the yellow star in the Free Zone. They had done more than accept; they had demanded the death of Feldman, Cavaillès, Politzer, Bourla, the deportation of Yvonne Picard, Péron, Kaan, Desnos. It was with these friends, dead or alive, that I felt solidarity; if I lifted a finger to help Brasillach, then it would have been their right to spit in my face.[53]

We would be remiss to read this passage as merely a personal reflection. Instead, Beauvoir touches on the core problem animating *The Ethics of Ambiguity*: the meanings and values we attach to actions are conflictual, contested, and must be "constantly won."[54] She denies that Brasillach is worthy of grief because the meaning of his actions is contained within the horizon of his active, fascist collaboration—for grief entails the mourning and commemoration of a loss. The claim that all lives ought to be grievable may be granted only in abstraction or as a demand for the recognition of an abstract right. In our practical lives we recognize that some lives—as the concatenation of an individual's actions and commitments—are not worthy of grief and, furthermore, that to grieve and commemorate the lives lost in the struggle for liberation obligates us to reject the grievability of their oppressors and enemies.[55]

DEMARCATING THE TERRAIN OF BUTLER'S POLITICS

I have reconstructed Beauvoir's views on interdependency and grief in order to show the limits of Butler's politics of grievability. In particular, I have aimed to demonstrate the narrow political horizon of the fundamental normative aspiration of

Butler's politics: the recognition of the equal grievability of all lives. Butler presents the recognition of vulnerability and inter-dependency as a corrective to contemporary social norms. This recognition would constitute the horizon for a new egalitarian vision that resists violence. Their politics translates into two spheres of practice. On the one hand, the politics of grievability may emerge as forms of protest and resistance that attempt to force—through the force of nonviolence, as it were—the recognition of ungrievable lives, such that they are recognized in the public sphere as grievable. On the other hand, grievability is formulated as a regulative ideal for world-building, that is, for reorganizing social infrastructures to safeguard social bonds.

We have not rejected Butler's politics outright. We have instead sought to demarcate its narrow terrain. One clear practical limit is demarcated by Beauvoir's reflections on grief. She shows that authentic grief for the victims of oppression entails the refusal of grief for their oppressors. In my view, then, Butler's politics is situated within a narrow terrain of recognition and redress. The demand that all lives ought to be grievable is directed specifically at governmental and social institutions that disavow the grievability of some lives. This judgement is confirmed by the base-building electoral politics evident in their essay "Protest, Violent and Nonviolent."

In sum, Butler's politics is locked into an opposition between some form of institutional biopolitics and resistance in the name of grievability. When we review the internal logic of Butler's politics, it is very similar to other iterations of nonviolent resistance. Here is the crucial point: if a political movement demands the recognition of grievability, then the use of violence *by that movement does indeed defeat* its political claim. Violence contradicts the performance of grievability by not extending grievability on an equal basis. *If* politics involves a demand to safeguard social bonds that mitigate social forms of vulnerability, then attacking social bonds contradicts that demand. As I have already mentioned, Butler's account aligns with standard justifications for nonviolent civil disobedience. However, if a social movement has a different goal, then this logic is not applicable. The goal of militant antifascism is to undermine the organizing capacity of far-right movements, and violence may facilitate that goal rather than contradict it. How violence fits within a diversity of tactics is a tactical or strategic question that must be handled by organizers on the ground.

Butler's politics is not merely restricted to protest. They also discuss the practice of world-building, which seeks to reorganize social relations around more egalitarian forms. Ultimately, it is when we consider world-building that the limitations of Butler's nonviolence are most obvious. Their philosophical framework is firmly anchored in a dichotomy between biopolitics and resistance. In this sense, the world that Butler believes we ought to build is an egalitarian alternative to the violent world of biopolitics. The first limitation becomes obvious when we consider social space as a contested ground of a three way fight, between a militant and revolutionary antifascist left, capitalism (with its liberal accoutrements), and the far right. I take it for granted that oppressed communities do not wait for social institutions to recognize them before they organize, which may include constructing egalitarian spaces of care, grievability, and the mitigation of social vulnerability. Because Butler's politics is grounded in recognition, they do not explore radical and revolutionary spaces that do not seek state or institutional recognition, nor do they explore how these organizing spaces need to defend themselves from hostile social forces. These spaces, on Butler's account, do not have justified recourse to emancipatory community self-defense, and thus by default they have no recourse other than law enforcement and the legal system. However, if such a community organizes in direct antagonism to the police, then they are either excluded from Butler's vision of egalitarian world-building or they lack recourse to any defense at all. What *force* can nonviolence truly have if it cannot protect embattled communities?

On this point, I believe a comparison with Beauvoir is instructive. She recognizes—as an existential description of the concept—that interdependency is a condition for both collective action and oppression, for it is the actions of others that extend and consolidate *or* stifle and frustrate my projects. However *recognition is not the goal of politics itself.* Politics entails the struggle for liberation, the expansion of the margin of freedom until the "realm of freedom," as Marx phrases it, is realized. Therefore, it would be self-defeating to refrain from protecting egalitarian spaces when they are attacked by hostile social forces. When we consider interdependency, vulnerability, and grievability as social forms that are integral to organizing, which must be protected in order to advance political struggle, then these concepts seem to necessitate a robust concept of community self-defense rather than an obligation to nonviolence.

5. THE PROBLEM OF LICENSING VIOLENCE

I have sought to discover, through a process of elimination, Butler's grounding justification for their principled rejection of violent tactics, which include a diversity of tactics and emancipatory community self-defense. Though this has required us to pursue a circuitous route to the conclusion, we have been able to defend two important counter-arguments to Butler. First, we have seen that not only does Butler's critique of the "self" of self-defense not apply to emancipatory community self-defense, but that advocates of the latter have already undertaken a similar self-critique to differentiate their efforts from common-sense notions of self-defense. Second, we have outlined a comparative reading of Butler and Beauvoir to show that concepts of interdependency and grievability—when applied to the social struggles of embattled communities—may warrant the use of violence rather than necessitating nonviolence.

Now there remains only the problem of license. Butler makes several claims about license, which I will differentiate as two separate theses. Their "weak" thesis is: the use and legitimation of violent action licenses others to use violence. Their "strong" thesis is: the use of violence *necessarily* leads to making the world a more violent place. With these two theses on license in mind, we may review Butler's actual claims. I will start with two examples from *The Force of Nonviolence*. The first presents the weak thesis: "the actualization of violence as a means can inadvertently become its own end, producing new violence, producing violence anew, reiterating the license, and licensing further violence" (20). The second presents the strong thesis: "the use of violence *only* makes the world into a more violent place, by bringing more violence into the world" (20, my emphasis).

I think it is important to note that there are many cases within the history of armed civil rights struggles that refute Butler's strong thesis.[56] However, because Butler does not appeal to historical evidence for either thesis, we will proceed through philosophical refutation.

We may quickly dispense with the strong thesis, ironically enough, on the basis of Butler's own text. Though they claim at points that violence *only* produces a more violent world, and that "violence operates as an intensification of social inequality" (142), they also admit a weaker claim that "*most* forms of violence are committed to inequality, whether or not that commitment is explicitly thematized" (57, my emphasis). Butler concedes that *not all* forms of violence are committed to social inequality, and hence, that they may *not* produce a more violent world.

Let us turn now to the weak thesis. I will introduce a more complex formulation of the weak thesis, because it also belies how liberal antifascists unwittingly fetishize violence. In "Protest, Violent and Nonviolent," Butler writes:

> What might at first seem to be a mere instrument to be discarded when its goal is accomplished turns out to be a praxis, a means that posits an end at the moment it is actualized; the means of violence posits violence as its

end. In other words, through making use of violence as
a means, one makes the world into a more violent place,
one brings more violence into the world. One violence
would have to be radically distinguished from another
if the violence the left protestors use were to be distinguished from the violence they condemn. But violence,
sadly, knows no such distinction.

As this passage indicates, Butler's ultimate objection to militant
antifascism (those vague "left protestors") is that some of its tactics would create a more violent world. Such a conclusion isn't
warranted by examining the explicit aim of antifascism, which is
to undermine far-right organizing. When Butler refers to means
and ends, they are relating means, not to a concrete goal, but
to a hypothetical world that such means would create. Indeed,
I believe the reference to means and ends hinders their argument. Instead, I think it is much clearer when Butler frames
the issue as one of license: i.e., when I use violence as a means,
I license others to use violence as a means to accomplish their
ends; therefore, I license a more violent world.

   Contra Butler, we must examine this supposed license for
violence in concrete terms. If it is correct that the current conjuncture involves a three way fight between militant antifascism,
capitalism and state power, and far-right movements, then we
must disentangle how each social force justifies violence.

   Fascism is the emblematic form of far-right social movements, and in many ways it illuminates the far-right valorization
of violence. As Stanislav Vysotsky writes:

Violence is central to fascist ideology as both a means
of achieving the world of inequality, hierarchy, and
domination they envision, and as the end result of a
world where that domination is produced and reproduced through explicit force. For fascists, violent
action is a moral good in and of itself, and it defines the
fascist as superior to his ideological opponents. The

fascist is morally and spiritually a better person because he is willing to impose his will through force.[57]

In addition, fascists do not merely consider violence a moral
good; as Walter Benjamin pointed out in the 1930s, they also
venerate it as an aesthetic object.[58] Here, we have a concrete
case of a social movement that venerates violence and does in
fact envision a more violent world. Fascists sometimes allege
that they are violent merely because left-wing activists "did it
first," which is a form of rhetorical dissimulation aimed at undermining liberal antifascist sympathy for militant antifascism.
Furthermore, they are well aware that increased law enforcement attention puts pressure on organizing, and when that pressure is applied to militant leftist formations it opens new opportunities for fascist organizing. It is an obligation of left-wing
intellectuals to dispel far-right dissimulation, an obligation that
Butler fails to meet.

Butler is certainly aware of the dissimulation of violence
by state power. They note that state power categorizes nonviolent resistance as violent, not on the basis of any particular action, but because it calls into question the legitimacy of state
policies or forms of rule (139–40). Against this dissimulation,
they prioritize "secur[ing] the semantics" of nonviolence, precisely because they need an unambiguous egalitarian norm to
justify nonviolent resistance practices (139). Therefore, when
the dominant frame casts nonviolent actions as violent, "then it
becomes all the more important to situate that naming practice
critically within political frameworks and their self-justificatory
schemes" (140). In other words, Butler believes that the critical task is to demonstrate how the dominant frame dissimulates
what is and isn't violence. Their desire to secure the semantics
of nonviolence — "to identify violence in a way that is clear and
commands consensus" (5) — not only aligns with the norms of
liberal antifascism but also demonstrates how those norms can
undermine militant political struggle. If the crucial task is to
distinguish legitimate nonviolent resistance from illegitimate

violent militancy, then, in effect, Butler is constructing a philo-sophical framework for policing the boundaries between good protestors and bad.[59] Indeed, they distance themself from left militancy because it appears to them a threat to securing a clear consensus about violence in the public sphere.

To return to the problem of license: Butler contends that the legitimation of violence functions somewhat like a Kantian maxim: when I use violence, I will that others may also use vio-lence. The foregoing discussion of the far right and capitalist state power shows instead that these social forces contending in the three way fight have, at least from their respective ide-ological perspectives, internally coherent (though not neces-sarily legitimate) justifications for violence. Butler argues that violence contains the potential to overwhelm its specific justi-fications or the intentions of those who use it, and thus "vio-lence, sadly, knows no such distinction[s]."[60] It is ironic that a philosopher whose work is firmly indebted to the poststruc-turalist critique of the subject appears to endow violence with an autonomous, sovereign agency. Violence, in these rhetori-cal flourishes, is an instance of what Marx refers to as a fetish: definite relations between contending social forces appear as an autonomous force which then interacts with humans and other things. Butler's fixation on license is a logical abstraction from the concrete bases of violence: violence is not an autono-mous agent; it is the product of concrete social forces, human agents who use violence, and the social conditions which en-able violence, which are enabled by it, or which constrain it. In his preface to this book, Michael Staudenmaier raises concrete concerns about the unintended consequences of the use of vio-lence by militant antifascists. Here, my critique focuses on the specific concept of license put forward by Butler.

6. EMANCIPATORY COMMUNITY SELF-DEFENSE

To conclude, we will return the problem of self-defense. Butler refuses to distinguish between oppressive violence and emancipatory violence (sometimes also referred to as revolutionary violence or counter-violence), a distinction which is made by revolutionaries and militants to contest the categorization, made by the ruling class, of the protection of social order as "force" and antagonism toward that order as "violence." Although there are numerous problems with his work, Georges Sorel succinctly captures this distinction: "the object of force is to impose a certain social order in which the minority governs, while violence tends to the destruction of that order. The bourgeoisie have used force since the beginning of modern times, while the proletariat now reacts against the middle class and against the State by violence."[61] I would contend that the dichotomy between force and violence is the concrete, stable semantic distinction that Butler seeks. Furthermore, I would contend it remains stable because it is a constant discursive structure of class domination. The class rule of the bourgeoisie justifies force as the application of objective right, and one critical task is to show how so-called objective right is both the rule of particular class interests and the imposition of concrete forms of systemic violence. Butler's solution, which is to carve out a space of nonviolent resistance between force and violence, leaves the underlying dichotomy unchallenged.

To conclude, I will defend militant antifascism as a form of emancipatory community self-defense. I will not develop a fulsome concept of emancipatory community self-defense here.[62] Instead, the discussion is narrowly tailored to anticipate and respond to two potential objections from Butler. First, I will argue that emancipatory community self-defense does not inadvertently license far-right and fascist violence. Then, second, I will show that emancipatory community self-defense is *emancipatory* because it seeks to protect embattled communities from hostile social forces without appealing to law enforcement.

WHY JUDITH BUTLER IS WRONG ABOUT MILITANT ANTIFASCISM

In other words, I will reframe the previous discussion of self-defense within the three way fight.

THE FAR RIGHT IS ANTI-EMANCIPATORY

First and foremost, emancipatory community self-defense is a form of community practice that is fundamentally different from common-sense notions of self-defense. As I have defined it, the *common-sense notion of self-defense* conceives of self-defense within a political continuum that runs from individual right to state violence; it holds that *in the absence of* law enforcement, in the moment of an imminent threat, an individual has the right to protect person, property, and family. In effect, it is a private, individual right that is a temporary exception to the state's asserted monopoly on violence. From Butler's perspective, one might object: if it is correct that contemporary far-right movements are system-oppositional and have, to some degree, an antagonistic relationship with the police (see Chapter 2 "Between System-Loyal Vigilantism and System-Oppositional Violence"), are they not then an embattled community entitled to emancipatory community self-defense?

To respond to this objection, we must examine both (1) the ideological position of far-right groups themselves and (2) the relationship between their political objectives and the settler-colonial state structure. Due to its influence across the far right, a brief examination of the political ideology of the Patriot movement is instructive. The Patriot movement is well known for numerous conflicts with law enforcement. Furthermore, as Chip Berlet and Matthew N. Lyons observe,

> Throughout the late 1990s the Patriot and armed militia movements overlapped with a resurgent states' rights movement and a new "county supremacy" movement. There was a rapid growth of illegal so-called constitutionalist common-law courts, set up by persons claiming a nonexistent "sovereign" citizenship. These courts claimed jurisdiction over legal matters on the

county or state level and dismissed the U.S. judicial system as corrupt and unconstitutional.[63]

Despite their distrust of the U.S. federal government, the Patriot movement positions itself as true inheritor of the legacy of the American Revolution and the early republic. In addition, it upholds the Second Amendment as the bulwark against federal tyranny. We may observe that they frame their system-oppositional position as an antagonism between local and federal power, and they position their political goals as a return to the true basis of American political power.

We may also observe that, generally speaking, far-right groups seek to re-entrench the social and economic hierarchies that have historically enabled white social and economic mobility: the capitalist regime of private property, white supremacy, heteropatriarchy, ableism, and settler colonialism. Some currents are explicitly system-oppositional in the sense that they seek to overthrow existing governmental institutions, but they remain loyal to the settler-colonial project. In other words, far-right movements are anti-emancipatory. Thus, far-right movements may organize with some degree of antagonism to law enforcement, yet they still tend to ground their activity within common-sense notions of self-defense.

MILITANT ANTIFASCISM AS
EMANCIPATORY COMMUNITY SELF-DEFENSE
I have defined emancipatory community self-defense as follows:

> *Emancipatory community self-defense* fosters autonomy and solidarity for socially vulnerable groups; it is organized against the antagonism of police oppression, so there is no presumed continuum between community action and police power; this communal form of self-defense is often not protected by the "right" of self-defense extended by the state.

As we have seen, the fact that a group organizes community self-defense in antagonism to law enforcement is not sufficient to be considered emancipatory. There must be an organizational relation to socially vulnerable groups that construct spaces of community that foster autonomy or self-determination for members of embattled communities and mitigate social vulnerability through mutual aid or solidarity. Community self-defense is *emancipatory* when it protects or in turn constructs spaces of community (and social relations) which are more egalitarian than the present status quo in society.

I generally consider militant antifascism as a form of emancipatory community self-defense, sometimes due to its relationships with embattled communities, and sometimes—as Vysotsky's ethnographic research on militant antifascist groups shows—because militant antifascist groups arise as a conscious choice for self-defense organized by embattled communities themselves. Though Vysotsky indicates that the two militant antifascist groups he studied were generally racially homogenous (i.e., white), they demonstrated gender parity.[64] Regarding sexual orientation, he observes that "individuals who identify as Queer are highly represented in formal and informal antifa activity."[65] Members of queer, trans, and other marginalized communities come together to defend themselves from supremacist violence, and this is clearly reflected in the composition of some militant antifascist groups. When commentators describe militant antifascists as a bunch of intransigent white dudes—a description which in my own experience does not bear out—they not only seek to undermine militant work as the product of outside agitators who are not part of embattled communities, they also challenge the emancipatory character of a given form of community self-defense. Butler, too, raises these types of conjectural criticisms.

It is time to conclude with *The Force of Nonviolence*. Butler's fundamental claim against the use of violence is that it licenses a more violent world. I have defended militant antifascism as a form of emancipatory community self-defense that protects spaces constructed by embattled and socially vulnerable communities, and, furthermore, I have maintained that the loss of these spaces, if they are attacked by hostile social forces, results in an objectively less egalitarian and worse-off world. By defending a form of principled nonviolence, while admitting merely temporary exceptions for self-defense, Butler is unable to provide guidance for the protection of these spaces. By default, it seems, they expect law enforcement to intervene. However, if we are serious about the antagonism between embattled communities and law enforcement, this solution undermines the very safety of the communities with which Butler expresses solidarity. Embattled communities resort to self-defense precisely because law enforcement intervention intensifies their social vulnerability. Nonviolence has little force when the far right targets these communities. Emancipatory community self-defense provides an alternative. As long as they maintain that emancipatory community self-defense would bring more violence into the world, without examining how such emancipatory collective practices could prevent it, Judith Butler will remain wrong about militant antifascism.

NOTES

1. Judith Butler, "Why is the Idea of 'Gender' Provoking Backlash the World Over?" *The Guardian*, October 23, 2021. Butler has recently adopted they/them pronouns.

2. Judith Butler, *The Force of Nonviolence: An Ethico-Political Bind* (London: Verso, 2020), 1, 63. All subsequent in-text citations refer to this book.

3. scott crow, ed. *Setting Sights: Histories and Reflections on Community and Armed Self-Defense* (Oakland: PM Press, 2018).

4. The most detailed critique is Alexander Livingston, "Inventing Nonviolence," *Boston Review*, August 31, 2020.

5. S. Shankar, "S. Shankar Reviews *The Force of Nonviolence*," *Critical Inquiry*, July 8, 2020.

6. Natasha Lennard, "Quiet Riot: A Philosopher's Argument for Nonviolent Resistance," *Bookforum*, September–November 2020.

7. I am borrowing the metaphor of terrain from J. Moufawad-Paul's *Demarcation and Demystification: Philosophy and Its Limits* (Winchester: Zer0 Books, 2019), 40ff.

8. Stanislav Vysotsky, *American Antifa: The Tactics, Culture, and Practice of Militant Antifascism* (London: Routledge, 2021), 2.

9. See Judith Butler, "Protest, Violent and Nonviolent," *Public Books*, October 13, 2017.

10. Butler, "Protest, Violent and Nonviolent."

11. Judith Butler, *Gender Trouble: Feminism and the Subversion of Identity* (New York: Routledge, 1990), 6.

12. Vysotsky, *American Antifa*, 88–89.

13. Roxanne Dunbar-Ortiz, *Loaded: A Disarming History of the Second Amendment* (San Francisco: City Lights Books, 2018), 26.

14. Dunbar-Ortiz, *Loaded*, 25.

15. Gina Starblanket and Dallas Hunt, *Storying Violence: Unravelling Colonial Narratives in the Stanley Trial* (Winnipeg: ARP Books, 2020), 67.

16. Elsa Dorlin, *Self-Defense: A Philosophy of Violence*, trans. Kieran Aarons (London: Verso, 2022), xviii.

17. Robert F. Williams, *Negroes with Guns* (Detroit: Wayne State University Press, 1998), 78.

18. Chad Kautzer, "Notes for a Critical Theory of Community Self-Defense," in *Setting Sights: Histories and Reflections on Community and Armed Self-Defense*, ed. scott crow (Oakland: PM Press, 2018), 35.

19. Robert F. Williams was influential on the subsequent armed Black freedom struggle, but as later groups noted, he organized local self-defense while appealing to the federal government to implement civil rights protections.

20. Frantz Fanon, *Toward the African Revolution*, trans. Haakon Chevalier (New York: Grove Press, 1988), 87.

21. In an interview, Butler states: "You know when I think it started for me? Here in the United States, during the AIDS crisis, when it became clear that many people were losing their lovers and not receiving adequate recognition for that loss. In many cases, people would go home to their families and try to explain their loss, or be unable to go home to their families or workplaces and try to explain their loss." See Masha Gessen, "Judith Butler Wants Us to Reshape Our Rage," *The New Yorker*, February 9, 2020.

22. Judith Butler, "Beauvoir on Sade: Making Sexuality into an Ethic," in *The Cambridge Companion to Simone de Beauvoir*, ed. Claudia Card (Cambridge: Cambridge University Press, 2003), 168–88; "Violence, Nonviolence: Sartre on Fanon," in *Race after Sartre: Antiracism, Africana Existentialism, Postcolonialism*, ed. Jonathan Judaken (Albany: SUNY Press, 2008), 211–31.

23. See Butler, *Gender Trouble*, 12; Genevieve Lloyd, *The Man of Reason: "Male" and "Female" in Western Philosophy* (Minneapolis: University of Minnesota Press, 1993), 101; Toril Moi, *Simone de Beauvoir: The Making of an Intellectual Woman* (Cambridge, Mass.: Blackwell, 1994), 142–44.

24. Sonia Kruks, "Beauvoir and the Marxism Question," in *A Companion to Simone de Beauvoir*, ed. Laura Hengehold and

Nancy Bauer (New Jersey: John Wiley and Sons, 2017), 236. Kruks points out that there is a political dimension to this neglect of Beauvoir's engagement with Marxism: "Later anglophone feminists, especially in the United States, have been increasingly dismissive of, indeed often hostile to, Marxism. For many, the Marxist aspects of Beauvoir's thinking are thus a source of considerable discomfort. Accordingly, they prefer to read her selectively, simply ignoring these aspects or assuming they are merely peripheral to her theory." Kruks, 238.

25. Judith Butler, *Precarious Life: The Powers of Mourning and Violence* (London: Verso, 2004), 29.

26. Butler, *Precarious Life*, 27.

27. Ruth Wilson Gilmore, *Golden Gulag: Prisons, Surplus, Crisis, and Opposition in Globalizing California* (Berkeley: University of California Press, 2007), 28.

28. Butler makes a curious concession that confirms this interpretation: "One of the strongest arguments for the use of violence on the left is that it is tactically necessary in order to defeat structural systemic violence … that may well be right, and I don't dispute it" (12–13) —though they then immediately do attempt to dispute the point.

29. Judith Butler, *Precarious Life*, 37.

30. Gessen, "Judith Butler Wants Us to Reshape Our Rage."

31. Livingston, "Inventing Nonviolence."

32. Here my terminological choices follow Kristana Arp, who writes: "Beauvoir calls these two types of freedom 'natural freedom' and 'moral freedom.' Instead of using the phrase 'natural freedom,' which is potentially misleading, I will refer to this first type of freedom as 'ontological freedom.' (There is no freedom in nature, after all, and no such thing as human nature for existentialism.)" See Arp, *The Bonds of Freedom: Simone de Beauvoir's Existentialist Ethics* (Chicago: Open Court, 2001), 55.

33. Jean-Paul Sartre, "The Itinerary of a Thought," *Between Existentialism and Marxism*, trans. John Matthews (London: Verso, 2008), 34.

34. Simone de Beauvoir, *The Force of Circumstance*, trans. Richard Howard (New York: Penguin Books, 1965), 76.

35. Simone de Beauvoir, *The Ethics of Ambiguity*, trans. Bernard Frechtman (New York: Open Road Integrated Media, 2018), 24, translation modified (hereafter abbreviated as "tm").

36. Beauvoir, *The Ethics of Ambiguity*, 80.

37. Beauvoir, *The Ethics of Ambiguity*, 25.

38. Beauvoir, *The Ethics of Ambiguity*, 88–89, tm.

39. See Thomas R. Flynn, *Sartre and Marxist Existentialism: The Test Case of Collective Responsibility* (Chicago: University of Chicago Press), 20; Sartre, *Being and Nothingness*, 483. Sartre writes: "Conflict is the original meaning of being-for-the-Other."

40. Beauvoir, *The Ethics of Ambiguity*, 83, tm.

41. By contrast, for Beauvoir, one may treat another as a means non-exploitatively if one another's ends are reciprocally recognized.

42. As an illustration, see Beauvoir's discussion of the "serious" colonial bureaucrat in *The Ethics of Ambiguity*, 52–54.

43. Beauvoir, *The Ethics of Ambiguity*, 108, 110–111.

44. Simone de Beauvoir, *The Second Sex*, trans. Constance Borde and Sheila Malovany-Chevallier (New York: Vintage Books, 2011), 644.

45. Beauvoir, *The Ethics of Ambiguity*, 89.

46. Beauvoir, *The Ethics of Ambiguity*, 19, tm.

47. Sartre, *Search for a Method*, trans. Hazel E. Barnes (New York: Vintage, 1968), 34, tm; Marx, *Capital*, vol. 3, trans. David Fernbach (London: Penguin,1991), 958–59.

48. Marx, *Capital*, vol. 3, 959.

49. See also Sonia Kruks, "Beauvoir and the Marxism Question," 236–38.

50. Beauvoir, "An Eye for an Eye," in *Philosophical Writings*, ed. Margaret A. Simons with Marybeth Timmermann and Mary Beth Mader (Urbana: University of Illinois Press, 2004), 250.

51. Beauvoir, "An Eye for an Eye," 246.

52. Beauvoir, "An Eye for an Eye," 258.

53. Beauvoir, *The Force of Circumstance*, 28–29.

54. Beauvoir, *The Ethics of Ambiguity*, 139.

55. Here I think of Kdog's anti-obituary for Tom Metzger, "American Strasser," *Three Way Fight*, December 9, 2020. Also included in Xtn Alexander and Matthew N. Lyons, eds., *Three Way Fight: Revolutionary Politics and Antifascism* (Montreal/Oakland: Kersplebedeb/PM Press, 2024), 125–33.

56. See, for example, Charles C. Cobb, Jr., *This Nonviolent Stuff'll Get You Killed: How Guns Made the Civil Rights Movement Possible* (Durham: Duke University Press, 2016); Lance Hill, *The Deacons for Defense: Armed Civil Resistance and the Civil Rights Movement* (Chapel Hill: University of North Carolina Press, 2004); Akinyele Omowale Umoja, *We Will Shoot Back: Armed Resistance in the Mississippi Freedom Movement* (New York: New York University Press, 2013).

57. Vysotsky, *American Antifa*, 85.

58. Walter Benjamin, "The Work of Art in the Age of Its Technological Reproducibility," in *Selected Writings*, vol. 3:

1935–1938, ed. Howard Eiland and Michael W. Jennings (New Haven: Belknap, 2002), 121.

59. M. I. Asma, *On Necrocapitalism: A Plague Journal* (Montreal: Kersplebedeb, 2021), 109–17.

60. Butler, "Protest, Violent and Nonviolent."

61. Georges Sorel, *Reflections on Violence*, ed. Jeremy Jennings (Cambridge: Cambridge University Press, 1999), 165–66.

62. For more detailed discussions, see my *Philosophy of Antifascism*, the essays collected in crow, *Setting Sights*, and Williams, *Negroes with Guns*.

63. Chip Berlet and Matthew N. Lyons, *Right-Wing Populism in America: Too Close for Comfort* (New York: Guilford Press, 2000), 292–93. See also Lyons's more recent *Insurgent Supremacists: The U.S. Far Right's Challenge to State and Empire* (Montreal/Oakland: Kersplebedeb/PM Press, 2018), 41–55.

64. Although, he adds, "While Jewish people are incorporated into white identity in the United States, their status is often considered one of 'conditional whiteness' because it may be revoked if the majority of white people decide to racialize Jewishness as an 'other,' as history has often demonstrated. Jewish people are often drawn to antifascist activity for reasons similar to members of other historically marginalized groups—because they are targets of supremacist violence." Vysotsky, *American Antifa*, 53.

65. He continues: "In my formal interviews with militant antifascists, exactly half of the sample identified as Lesbian, Gay, or Bisexual. During my time observing New City Antifa [a pseudonym], roughly one-third of members identified as Queer with representation growing to one half shortly after the end of the formal ethnographic research period." See Vysotsky, *American Antifa*, 53.

Bibliography

Abu-Jamal, Mumia. *We Want Freedom: A Life in the Black Panther Party.* Cambridge, Mass.: South End Press, 2004.

Alexander, Xtn, and Matthew N. Lyons, eds. *Three Way Fight: Revolutionary Politics and Antifascism.* Montreal/Oakland: Kersplebedeb/PM Press, 2024.

Arp, Kristana. *The Bonds of Freedom: Simone de Beauvoir's Existentialist Ethics.* Chicago: Open Court, 2001.

Asma, M. I. *On Necrocapitalism: A Plague Journal.* Montreal: Kersplebedeb, 2021.

Beauvoir, Simone de. "An Eye for an Eye." In *Philosophical Writings*, ed. Margaret A. Simons with Marybeth Timmermann and Mary Beth Mader. Urbana: University of Illinois Press, 2004, 245–60.

Beauvoir, Simone de. *The Ethics of Ambiguity*, trans. Bernard Frechtman. New York: Open Road Integrated Media, 2018.

Beauvoir, Simone de. *The Force of Circumstance*, trans. Richard Howard. New York: Penguin Books, 1965.

Beauvoir, Simone de. *The Second Sex*, trans. Constance Borde and Sheila Malovany-Chevallier. New York: Vintage Books, 2011.

Bello, Walden. *Counterrevolution: The Global Rise of the Far Right.* Black Point, Nova Scotia: Fernwood, 2019.

Benjamin, Walter. "The Work of Art in the Age of Its Technological Reproducibility." In *Selected Writings*, vol. 3: 1935–1938, edited by Howard Eiland and Michael W. Jennings. New Haven: Belknap, 2002, 101–33.

Berlet, Chip, and Matthew N. Lyons. *Right-Wing Populism in America: Too Close for Comfort*. New York: Guilford Press, 2000.

The Black Panther Party. "Call for a United Front against Fascism." In *The U.S. Antifascism Reader*, edited by Bill V. Mullen and Christopher Vials. London: Verso, 2020, 267–69.

Boggs, James. *Racism and the Class Struggle: Further Pages from a Black Worker's Notebook*. New York: Monthly Review Press, 1970.

Bray, Mark. *Antifa: The Anti-fascist Handbook*. New York: Melville House, 2017.

Bromma. *The Worker Elite: Notes on the "Labor Aristocracy"*. Montreal: Kersplebedeb, 2014.

Bruyneel, Kevin. *Settler Memory: The Disavowal of Indigeneity and the Politics of Race in the United States*. Chapel Hill: UNC Press, 2021.

Burley, Shane. *Why We Fight: Essays on Fascism, Resistance, and Surviving the Apocalypse*. Chico: AK Press, 2021.

Butler, Judith. "Beauvoir on Sade: Making Sexuality into an Ethic." In *The Cambridge Companion to Simone de Beauvoir*, edited by Claudia Card. Cambridge: Cambridge University Press, 2003, 168–88.

Butler, Judith. *The Force of Nonviolence: An Ethico-Political Bind*. London: Verso, 2020.

Butler, Judith. *Gender Trouble: Feminism and the Subversion of Identity*. New York: Routledge, 1990.

Butler, Judith. *Precarious Life: The Powers of Mourning and Violence*. London: Verso, 2004.

Butler, Judith. "Protest, Violent and Nonviolent." *Public Books*, October 13, 2017. https://www.publicbooks.org/the-big-picture-protest-violent-and-nonviolent/

Butler, Judith. "Violence, Nonviolence: Sartre on Fanon." In *Race after Sartre: Antiracism, Africana Existentialism, Postcolonialism*, edited by Jonathan Judaken. Albany: SUNY Press, 2008, 211–31.

Butler, Judith. "Why is the Idea of 'Gender' Provoking Backlash the World Over?" *The Guardian*, October 23, 2021. https://www.theguardian.com/us-news/commentisfree/2021/oct/23/judith-butler-gender-ideology-backlash

Clay, Shannon, Lady, Kristin Schwartz, and Michael Staudenmaier. *We Go Where They Go: The Story of Anti-Racist Action*. Oakland: PM Press, 2023.

Cleaver, Kathleen. "Racism, Fascism, and Political Murder." In Bill V. Mullen and Christopher Vials, eds., *The U.S. Antifascism Reader*. London: Verso, 2020, 260–66.

Cobb, Jr., Charles E. *This Nonviolent Stuff'll Get You Killed: How Guns Made the Civil Rights Movement Possible*. Durham: Duke University Press, 2016.

Communist Working Circle, ed. *V. I. Lenin: On Imperialism and Opportunism*. Montreal: Kersplebedeb, 2019.

crow, scott, ed. *Setting Sights: Histories and Reflections on Community and Armed Self-Defense*. Oakland: PM Press, 2018.

Cunningham, David. *There's Something Happening Here: The New Left, the Klan, and FBI Counterintelligence*. University of California Press, 2005.

Derbent, T. *Categories of Revolutionary Military Policy.* Montreal: Kersplebedeb, 2006. http://urbanguerilla.org/categories-of-revolutionary-military-policy-t-derbent-april-2006/

Derbent, T. *The German Communist Resistance 1933–1945.* Paris: Foreign Languages Press, 2021.

Dimitrov, George. *The Fascist Offensive and Unity of the Working Class.* Paris: Foreign Languages Press, 2020.

Dorlin, Elsa. *Self-Defense: A Philosophy of Violence,* trans. Kieran Aarons. London: Verso, 2022.

Du Bois, W.E.B. "The African Roots of War." *Monthly Review* 24, no. 11 (1973): 28–40.

Du Bois, W.E.B. *Black Reconstruction in America: An Essay Toward a History of the Part Which Black Folk Played in the Attempt to Reconstruct Democracy in America, 1860–1880,* edited by Henry Louis Gates, Jr. Oxford: Oxford University Press, 2007.

Du Bois, W.E.B. "Marxism and the Negro Problem." In *Writings in Periodicals Edited by W.E.B. Du Bois: Selections from The Crisis,* vol. 2: 1926–1934, edited by Herbert Aptheker. Millwood, NY: Kraus-Thomson, 1983, 695–99.

Dunbar-Ortiz, Roxanne. *Loaded: A Disarming History of the Second Amendment.* San Francisco: City Lights Books, 2018.

Eco, Umberto. "Ur-Fascism." *The New York Review of Books,* June 22, 1995. https://www.nybooks.com/articles/1995/06/22/ur-fascism/

Evans, Robert. "The Boogaloo Movement Is Not What You Think." bellingcat, May 27, 2020. https://www.bellingcat.com/news/2020/05/27/the-boogaloo-movement-is-not-what-you-think/

Fanon, Frantz. *Toward the African Revolution*, trans. Haakon Chevalier. New York: Grove Press, 1988.

Faulders, Katherine, Justin Fishel, and Alexander Mallin. "Trump, Barr Tell Governors to 'Dominate' Streets in Response to Unrest." abcnews, June 1, 2020. https://abcnews.go.com/Politics/trump-barr-governors-dominate-streets-response-unrest/story?id=70994362

Flynn, Thomas R. *Sartre and Marxist Existentialism: The Test Case of Collective Responsibility.* Chicago: University of Chicago Press.

Fronczak, Joseph. *Everything is Possible: Antifascism and the Left in the Age of Fascism.* New Haven: Yale University Press, 2023.

Gandesha, Samir. "Posthuman Fascism." *Los Angeles Review of Books*, August 22, 2020. https://lareviewofbooks.org/article/posthuman-fascism/

Gessen, Masha. "Judith Butler Wants Us to Reshape Our Rage." *The New Yorker*, February 9, 2020. https://www.newyorker.com/culture/the-new-yorker-interview/judith-butler-wants-us-to-reshape-our-rage

Gilmore, Ruth Wilson. *Golden Gulag: Prisons, Surplus, Crisis, and Opposition in Globalizing California.* Berkeley: University of California Press, 2007.

Griffin, Roger. *The Nature of Fascism.* London: Pinter Publishers, 1991.

Hamerquist, Don. *A Brilliant Red Thread: Revolutionary Writings from Don Hamerquist*, edited by Luis Brennan. Montreal: Kersplebedeb, 2023.

Hamerquist, Don. "Fascism and Anti-Fascism." In Don Hamerquist, et al. *Confronting Fascism: Discussion Documents for a Militant Movement*, 2nd edition. Montreal: Kersplebedeb, 2017, 27–93.

Harris, Cheryl. "Whiteness as Property." *Harvard Law Review* 106, no. 8 (June 1993): 1707–91.

Hill, Lance. *The Deacons for Defense: Armed Civil Resistance and the Civil Rights Movement.* Chapel Hill: University of North Carolina Press, 2004.

Ignatiev, Noel (writing as Noel Ignatin). "Fascism: Some Common Misconceptions." *Urgent Tasks* 4 (Summer 1978): 25–32.

Kdog. "American Strasser." *Three Way Fight* (website), December 9, 2020. https://threewayfight.blogspot.com/2020/12/american-strasser.html

Kautzer, Chad. "Notes for a Critical Theory of Community Self-Defense." In *Setting Sights: Histories and Reflections on Community and Armed Self-Defense*, edited by scott crow. Oakland: PM Press, 2018, 35–48.

Kelley, Robin D.G. *Hammer and Hoe: Alabama Communists during the Great Depression*, 25th anniversary edition. Chapel Hill: UNC Press, 2015.

Kinshasa, Kwando Mbiassi. *Black Resistance to the Ku Klux Klan in the Wake of the Civil War.* Jefferson, NC: McFarland and Co., 2006.

Kovich, Tammy, El Jones, Veronica L., Butch Lee, *Anti-Fascism against Machismo.* Montreal: Kersplebedeb, 2023.

Kruks, Sonia. "Beauvoir and the Marxism Question." In *A Companion to Simone de Beauvoir*, ed. Laura Hengehold and Nancy Bauer. New Jersey: John Wiley and Sons, 2017, 236–48.

Lauesen, Torkil. *The Global Perspective: Reflections on Imperialism and Resistance.* Montreal: Kersplebedeb, 2018.

Lawrence, Ken. "The Ku Klux Klan and Fascism." *Urgent Tasks* 14 (Fall/Winter 1982): 12–16. Reprinted in Bill V.

Mullen and Christopher Vials, eds., *The U.S. Anti-fascism Reader.* London: Verso, 2020, 289–299.

Lee, Butch. *Jailbreak Out of History: The Re-Biography of Harriet Tubman and "The Evil of Female Loaferism."* Montreal: Kersplebedeb, 2015.

Lee, Butch. *The Military Strategy of Women and Children.* Montreal: Kersplebedeb, 2003.

Lee, Butch, and Red Rover. *Night-Vision: Illuminating War and Class on Neo-Colonial Terrain.* Montreal: Kersplebedeb, 2017.

Lenin, V. I. "The Collapse of the Second International." In *Collected Works* 21. Moscow: Progress Publishers, 1960–1970, 205–59.

Lenin, V. I. "Imperialism and the Split in Socialism." In *Collected Works* 23. Moscow: Progress Publishers, 1960–1970, 105–20.

Lenin, V. I. *Imperialism, the Highest Stage of Capitalism.* Paris: Foreign Languages Press, 2020.

Lenin, V. I. "The Second Congress of the Communist International." In *Collected Works* 31. Moscow: Progress Publishers, 1960–1970, 212–63.

Lennard, Natasha. "Quiet Riot: A Philosopher's Argument for Nonviolent Resistance." *Bookforum*, September–November 2020. https://www.bookforum.com/print/2703/a-philosopher-s-argument-for-nonviolent-resistance-24173

Livingston, Alexander. "Inventing Nonviolence." *Boston Review*, August 31, 2020. https://bostonreview.net/articles/alexander-livingston-inventing-nonviolence/

Lloyd, Genevieve. *The Man of Reason: "Male" and "Female" in Western Philosophy.* Minneapolis: University of Minnesota Press, 1993.

Luxemburg, Rosa. *Reform or Revolution?* Paris: Foreign Languages Press, 2020.

Lyons, Matthew N. *Insurgent Supremacists: The U.S. Far Right's Challenge to State and Empire.* Montreal/Oakland: Kersplebedeb/PM Press, 2018.

Lyons, Matthew N. "Review of 'Anti-Fascism Beyond Machismo' by Petronella Lee." *Three Way Fight* (website), October 17, 2019. https://threewayfight.blogspot.com/2019/10/review-of-anti-fascism-beyond-machismo.html

Lyons, Matthew N. "Trump, the Far Right, and the Return of Vigilante Repression." *Three Way Fight* (website), September 1, 2020. https://threewayfight.blogspot.com/2020/09/trump-far-right-and-return-of-vigilante.html

Marx, Karl. *Capital*, vol. 3, trans. David Fernbach. London: Penguin,1991.

Marx, Karl. "The Civil War in France." In *The First International and After: Political Writings*, vol. 3, edited by David Fernbach. London: Penguin, 1974, 187–236.

Marx, Karl. "The Future Results of the British Rule in India," in *Surveys from Exile: Political Writings*, vol. 2, edited by David Fernbach. London: Penguin, 1973.

Miller, Cassie. "The 'Boogaloo' Started as a Racist Meme." SPLC, June 5, 2020. https://www.splcenter.org/hatewatch/2020/06/05/boogaloo-started-racist-meme

Moi, Toril. *Simone de Beauvoir: The Making of an Intellectual Woman.* Cambridge, Mass.: Blackwell, 1994.

Moore, Hilary, and James Tracy, *No Fascist USA! The John Brown Anti-Klan Committee and Lessons for Today's Movements.* San Francisco: City Lights, 2020.

Moufawad-Paul, J. *Demarcation and Demystification: Philosophy and Its Limits.* Winchester: Zer0 Books, 2019.

Murali, K. (Ajith). *Critiquing Brahmanism: A Collection of Essays.* Paris: Foreign Languages Press, 2020.

Pape, Robert A., and Chicago Project on Security and Threats. "Understanding American Domestic Terrorism: Mobilization Potential and Risk Factors of a New Threat Trajectory." Division of the Social Sciences, University of Chicago, April 6, 2021. https://d3qi0qp55mx5f5.cloudfront.net/cpost/i/docs/americas_insurrectionists_online_2021_04_06.pdf

Paxton, Robert O. *The Anatomy of Fascism.* New York: Vintage, 2004.

Political Research Associates. "Police, Paramilitaries, and Protests for Racial Justice." June 3, 2020. https://politicalresearch.org/2020/06/03/police-paramilitaries-and-protests-racial-justice

Poulantzas, Nicos. *Fascism and Dictatorship: The Third International and the Problem of Fascism,* trans. Judith White. London: Verso, 1979.

Riddell, John, ed. *Toward the United Front: Proceedings of the Fourth Congress of the Communist International, 1922.* Chicago: Haymarket Books, 2012.

Robinson, Rowland "Enāēmaehkiw" Keshena. "Fascism and Anti-Fascism: A Decolonial Perspective." *Maehkōn Ahpēhtesewen,* February 11, 2017 [Edited 2019]. https://onkwehonwerising.wordpress.com/2017/02/11/fascism-anti-fascism-a-decolonial-perspective

Roediger, David R. *The Wages of Whiteness: Race and the Making of the American Working Class,* revised edition. London: Verso, 1999.

Sakai, J. *The "Dangerous Class" and Revolutionary Theory: Thoughts on the Making of the Lumpen/proletariat.* Montreal: Kersplebedeb, 2017.

Sakai, J. *The Shape of Things to Come.* Montreal: Kersplebedeb, 2023.

Sakai, J. "The Shock of Recognition." In Don Hamerquist, et al. *Confronting Fascism: Discussion Documents for a Militant Movement*, 2nd edition. Montreal: Kersplebedeb, 2017, 95–197.

Sartre, Jean-Paul. *Being and Nothingness*, trans. Sarah Richmond. London: Routledge, 2018.

Sartre, Jean-Paul. "The Itinerary of a Thought." In *Between Existentialism and Marxism*, trans. John Matthews. London: Verso, 2008, 33–64.

Sartre, Jean-Paul. *Search for a Method*, trans. Hazel E. Barnes. New York: Vintage, 1968.

Shankar, S. "S. Shankar Reviews *The Force of Nonviolence*." *Critical Inquiry*, July 8, 2020. https://criticalinquiry.uchicago.edu/s.shankar_reviews_the_force_of_nonviolence

Shaw, D.Z. "From German Communist Antifascism to a Contemporary United Front," in T. Derbent, *The German Communist Resistance 1933–1945*. Paris: Foreign Languages Press, 2021, 1–18.

Shaw, D.Z., *Philosophy of Antifascism: Punching Nazis and Fighting White Supremacy*. London: Rowman and Littlefield International, 2020.

Snell, Robert, and Melissa Nann Burke. "Plans to Kidnap Whitmer, Overthrow Government Spoiled, Officials Say." *The Detroit News*, October 8, 2020. https://www.detroitnews.com/story/news/local/michigan/2020/10/08/feds-thwart-militia-plot-kidnap-michigan-gov-gretchen-whitmer/5922301002

Sonabend, Daniel. *We Fight Fascists: The 43 Group and Their Forgotten Battle for Post-war Britain*. London: Verso, 2019.

Sorel, Georges. *Reflections on Violence*, edited by Jeremy Jennings. Cambridge: Cambridge University Press, 1999.

Stanley, Jason. *How Fascism Works: The Politics of Us and Them.* New York: Random House, 2018.

Starblanket, Gina, and Dallas Hunt. *Storying Violence: Unravelling Colonial Narratives in the Stanley Trial.* Winnipeg: ARP Books, 2020.

Staudenmaier, Michael "Strange Bedfellows?" *Fifth Estate* 361 (Summer 2003). https://www.fifthestate.org/archive/361-summer-2003-2/strange-bedfellows/

Staudenmaier, Michael. *Truth and Revolution: A History of the Sojourner Truth Organization 1969–1986.* Oakland: AK Press, 2012.

Strether, Lambert. "The Class Composition of the Capitol Rioters (First Cut)." *Naked Capitalism*, January 18, 2021. https://www.nakedcapitalism.com/2021/01/the-class-composition-of-the-capitol-rioters-first-cut.html

Testa, M. *Militant Anti-fascism: A Hundred Years of Resistance.* Oakland: AK Press, 2015.

Toscano, Alberto. "'America's Belgium': W.E.B. Du Bois on Race, Class, and the Origins of World War I." In Alexander Anievas, ed. *Cataclysm 1914: The First World War and the Making of Modern Politics.* Chicago: Haymarket Books, 2016, 236–57.

Toscano, Alberto. "The Long Shadow of Racial Fascism." *Boston Review*, October 28, 2020. https://www.bostonreview.net/articles/long-shadow-racial-fascism

Traverso, Enzo. *The Jewish Question: History of a Marxist Debate.* Chicago: Haymarket Books, 2019.

Traverso, Enzo. *The New Faces of Fascism: Populism and the Far Right.* London: Verso, 2019.

Umoja, Akinyele Omowale. *We Will Shoot Back: Armed Resistance in the Mississippi Freedom Movement.* New York: New York University Press, 2013.

Vials, Christopher. *Haunted by Hitler: Liberals, the Left, and the Fight against Fascism in the United States.* Amherst: University of Massachusetts Press, 2014.

Vysotsky, Stanislav. *American Antifa: The Tactics, Culture, and Practice of Militant Antifascism.* London: Routledge, 2021.

Williams, Kristian. "U.S. Cops Are Treating White Militias as 'Heavily Armed Friendlies'." *Truthout*, September 17, 2020. https://truthout.org/articles/us-cops-are-treating-white-militias-as-heavily-armed-friendlies

Williams, Robert F. *Negroes with Guns.* Detroit: Wayne State University Press, 1998.

Winton, Richard, Maura Dolan, and Anita Chabria. "Far-right 'Boogaloo Boys' Linked to Killing of California Law Officers and Other Violence." *Los Angeles Times*, June 17, 2020. https://www.latimes.com/california/story/2020-06-17/far-right-boogaloo-boys-linked-to-killing-of-california-lawmen-other-violence

Zetkin, Clara. *Fighting Fascism: How to Struggle and How to Win*, edited by Mike Taber and John Riddell. Chicago: Haymarket Books, 2017.

Acknowledgements

I would like to thank Karl at Kersplebedeb for his ongoing interest in my work and for introducing me to the circle that does a lot of work for the Three Way Fight blog. The collective feedback from Matthew N. Lyons (whose editorial eye is unparalleled), Xtn, and Don Hamerquist prevented several blunders on my part and improved my writing. I should also extend my gratitude to the editors at Foreign Languages Press, who offered me an opportunity to preface T. Derbent's *The German Communist Resistance 1933–1945* and to contribute to the inaugural issue of *Material*. My work has also benefited from discussions with Stanislav Vysotsky, Joan Braune, and J. Moufawad-Paul. Finally, I would not be able to put the proverbial pen to paper without the constant support of my main comrade, kylie.

This book is dedicated to the memory of Andy Holman and Aaron Steichen, two comrades who went too soon.

About the Author

D.Z. Shaw teaches at a community college in so-called British Columbia. He is the author of *Philosophy of Antifascism: Punching Nazis and Fighting White Supremacy* (2020), *The Politics of the Blockade* (Kersplebedeb, 2020), *Egalitarian Moments: From Descartes to Rancière* (2016), and numerous essays on philosophy and political thought. He is one co-author in the multi-author collaboration published under the pseudonym M.I. Asma, *On Necrocapitalism: A Plague Journal* (Kersplebedeb, 2021). He is also a co-editor of the book series Living Existentialism, published by Rowman and Littlefield.

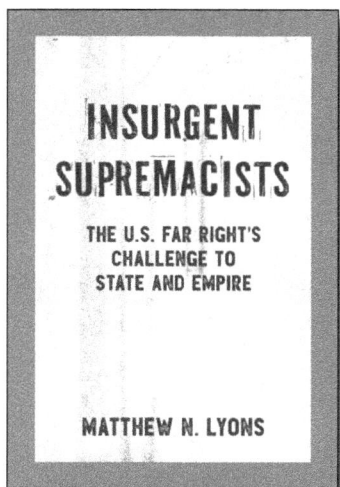

INSURGENT SUPREMACISTS: THE U.S. FAR RIGHT'S CHALLENGE TO STATE AND EMPIRE

MATTHEW N. LYONS

ISBN 9781629635118

384 PAGES

$24.95 USD

A major study of movements that strive to overthrow the U.S. government, that often claim to be anti-imperialist and sometimes even anti-capitalist, yet which also consciously promote inequality, hierarchy, and domination, generally along explicitly racist, sexist, and homophobic lines. Revolutionaries of the far right: insurgent supremacists.

In this book, Matthew N. Lyons takes readers on a tour of neo-nazis and Christian theocrats, by way of the patriot movement, the LaRouchites, and the alt-right. Supplementing this, thematic sections explore specific dimensions of far-right politics, regarding gender, decentralism, and anti-imperialism.

Intervening directly in debates within left and antifascist movements, Lyons examines both the widespread use and abuse of the term "fascism" and the relationship between federal security forces and the paramilitary right. His final chapter offers a preliminary analysis of the Trump presidential administration's relationship with far-right politics and the organized far right's shifting responses to it.

Both for its analysis and as a guide to our opponents, Insurgent Supremacists promises to be a powerful tool in organizing to resist the forces at the cutting edge of reaction today.

ANTIFASCISM AGAINST MACHISMO

TAMMY KOVICH, BUTCH LEE, VERONICA L., EL JONES

ISBN 9781989701232

162 PAGES

$12 USD

An intergenerational dialogue on the contours and content of feminist antifascism.

Four feminist, antifascist revolutionaries jump off from each other's reflections and bring the particularities of their varied contexts to bear on one central problem: What has and will a women's war against fascism look like?

In these times of rising instability, fracturing identities, and a resultant rise in challenges to and defences of white supremacist patriarchy, *Antifascism Against Machismo* makes a powerful contribution to the understanding needed for a revolutionary resistance at the same time as it offers a model for political discussion. Women building revolutionary theory together, between different contexts, across borders and generations, and beyond the stale fences of political sects.

ALSO FROM KERSPLEBEDEB

THREE WAY FIGHT: REVOLUTIONARY POLITICS AND ANTIFASCISM

**EDITED BY XTN ALEXANDER
& MATTHEW N. LYONS**

ISBN 9798887440415

416 PAGES

$24.95 USD

This book offers an introduction to the politics and practice of the three way fight, with more than thirty essays, position statements, and interviews from the Three Way Fight website and elsewhere, spanning from the antifascist struggles of the 1980s and 1990s to the political upheavals of the twenty-first century. Over fifteen authors explore a range of topics, such as fascist politics' relationship to patriarchy and settler colonialism, Tom Metzger's "Third Position" (anticapitalist) fascism, conflict within the business community over the 2016 presidential election, and the Trump administration's shifting relationship with the organized far right. Many of the writings address issues of political strategy, such as tensions between radicals and liberals within the reproductive rights movement and the George Floyd rebellion, video gaming as an arena of political struggle, and the importance (and challenges) of approaching antifascist organizing in ways that are militant, community based, and nonsectarian.

KER SPL EBE DEB

Since 1998 Kersplebedeb has been an important source of radical literature and agit prop materials.

The project has a non-exclusive focus on anti-patriarchal and anti-imperialist politics, framed within an anticapitalist perspective.
A special priority is given to writings regarding armed struggle in the metropole, the continuing struggles of political prisoners and prisoners of war, and the political economy of imperialism.

The Kersplebedeb website presents historical and contemporary writings by revolutionary thinkers from the anarchist and communist traditions.

Kersplebedeb can be contacted at:

Kersplebedeb
CP 63560
CCCP Van Horne
Montreal, Quebec
Canada
H3W 3H8

email: info@kersplebedeb.com
web: www.kersplebedeb.com
        www.leftwingbooks.net

Kersplebedeb

www.ingramcontent.com/pod-product-compliance
Lightning Source LLC
Chambersburg PA
CBHW062052270326
41931CB00013B/3039